THE LIBRARY OF
AMERICAN
LIVES AND TIMES™

STONEWALL JACKSON

Hero of the Confederacy

J. Tracy Power

The Rosen Publishing Group's
PowerPlus Books™
New York

For Dawn, Ginger, Jake, and Julia

Published in 2005 by The Rosen Publishing Group, Inc.
29 East 21st Street, New York, NY 10010

First Edition

*Editor's Note: All quotations have been reproduced as they appeared in
the letters and diaries from which they were borrowed. No correction was
made to the inconsistent spelling that was common in that time period.*

Library of Congress Cataloging-in-Publication Data

Power, J. Tracy.
Stonewall Jackson : hero of the confederacy / J. Tracy Power.
   v. cm.
Includes bibliographical references and index.
Contents: Who was Stonewall Jackson? — The making of a young man
— A cadet at West Point — War in Mexico — An Army officer and a
professor — Life in Lexington — The divided Union, a Civil War, and a
new name — "Oh, for a dozen Jacksons!" — "One of the greatest men
living" — Marching to glory — Stonewall Jackson and his legacy.
ISBN 1-4042-2654-0 (library binding)
1. Jackson, Stonewall, 1824–1863—Juvenile literature. 2. Generals—
Confederate States of America—Biography—Juvenile literature. 3.
Confederate States of America. Army—Biography—Juvenile litera-
ture. 4. United States—History—Civil War, 1861–1865—Campaigns—
Juvenile literature. [1. Jackson, Stonewall, 1824–1863. 2. Generals. 3.
United States—History—Civil War, 1861–1865.] I. Title.
E467.1.J15 P69 2005
973.7'3'092—dc21

                     2003007061
                        Rev.

Manufactured in the United States of America

CONTENTS

1. Who Was Stonewall Jackson?

He was a tall man, with brown hair, a mustache, a beard, and piercing blue eyes. He usually dressed in a plain, worn uniform and wore an old blue cap with its bill pulled down nearly over his nose. He rode a small horse that looked almost as worn as his uniform, and his long legs looked as if they might scrape the ground with every step the horse took. At thirty-nine years of age, he was at the height of his fame.

His name was Thomas Jonathan Jackson, but people across the South, the North, and the world soon came to know him as Stonewall. Jackson succeeded in spite of the odds stacked against him. His father and mother both died before Jackson was eight years old. He was raised by an uncle on an isolated farm. His early education was limited, and he was fortunate to win an appointment to the U.S. Military Academy at West

Opposite: John Adams Elder painted this portrait of Thomas Jonathan Jackson around 1863. Determined to defeat the enemy and to take advantage of every opportunity, Jackson often kept his plans secret from his own officers, marched his men past the point of exhaustion, and was impatient with anyone who did not live up to his standards.

Point, New York. There he studied and worked hard. After he graduated, he served as a soldier and a teacher. In 1861, when the country was divided by civil war, Jackson returned to the field as an officer in the Confederate army. He gained widespread recognition after the war's first major battle, and he became a Confederate hero after his brilliant campaign in the Shenandoah Valley of Virginia.

By the summer of 1862, Stonewall Jackson was the most popular person in the Confederacy. He was, as the Richmond, Virginia, *Dispatch* proclaimed, "beyond all question, the hero of the war." Articles about his generalship, his life before the war, and his habits were published in southern newspapers and were reprinted in northern and foreign publications. These articles were often inaccurate, exaggerated, or invented, contributing to his mythic status. Engravings of Jackson were printed in newspapers and magazines, based on photographs and on drawings by artists who traveled with the armies. Songs and poems recounting his heroic feats were popular, too.

Stonewall Jackson's brief career as a Confederate general would last only two years. During that time, he earned his place among the most famous generals in American history.

2. The Making of a Young Man

On January 21, 1824, Thomas Jackson was born in the small town of Clarksburg, Harrison County, Virginia, which today is in West Virginia. He was the third child of Jonathan and Julia Neale Jackson. The couple's first child, Elizabeth, had been born in 1819. Their second, a son named Warren, had been born in 1821.

In the spring of 1826, six-year-old Elizabeth was sick with typhoid fever, and Julia was about to give birth to her fourth child. Jonathan cared for his young daughter, but despite his efforts Elizabeth died. Soon Jonathan came down with the deadly fever, too. He died a few days later, at the age of thirty-six. The next day, Julia Jackson, a widow at the age of twenty-eight, gave birth to a daughter, whom she named Laura. Julia struggled to support her family. They lived in a small cottage, and Julia taught school and made a little money sewing for families in town.

Within a few years, Julia met Blake Woodson, a lawyer in Clarksburg. Woodson was fifteen years her senior and a widower with eight children of his own,

Jonathan Jackson was generous to a fault, irresponsible, and unlucky with money. He regularly signed promissory notes for family and friends, agreeing to pay back their loans if they could not. When these debtors defaulted on their loans, Jackson was responsible for their debts. He often borrowed money or sold some of his land to pay off these loans. He also gambled at cards, and he lost more than he won.

although none of them lived with him. Julia married Blake Woodson in 1830. By the following summer, Woodson had been appointed county clerk of Fayette County, about 90 miles (144.8 km) southwest of Clarksburg. He and his new family moved there and settled in the town of New Haven, later renamed Ansted. Unfortunately, Woodson was a poor businessman. He was soon in debt. Adding to the family's financial burdens, Julia announced that she was going to have a baby.

To help ease the financial strain on the family, Julia's eldest child, Warren, was sent to live with relatives in Parkersburg. At first, Thomas, known as Tom, and Laura remained in Ansted, but Julia soon decided that they, too, should live with relatives. They were sent to Jackson's Mill, an area named for the family's sawmill and gristmill.

That fall Julia and Blake Woodson welcomed a new baby into the family. The child was a healthy boy, but Julia, already ill from tuberculosis, became weaker every day. At their mother's request, Tom and Laura returned to Ansted. Julia died soon after, at the age of thirty-three. Blake Woodson either could not or did not want to take

When Julia Jackson announced that seven-year-old Tom and five-year-old Laura would be sent to Jackson's Mill, Tom ran into the woods to hide in protest. Only after dark, when his mother and an uncle begged him to come inside, did he finally reappear. Tom Jackson's boyhood home at Jackson's Mill was photographed in 1909, by William A. Ball.

care of Tom and Laura, and the two young children were sent back to Jackson's Mill.

Jackson's Mill was home to Tom and Laura's step-grandmother, Elizabeth Jackson, and her six sons and two daughters, who were loving uncles and aunts. Elizabeth's eldest son, Cummins Jackson, was twenty-nine years old when the children came to live at the mill. He ran the farm, the sawmill, and the gristmill. He had many friends, but he had a short temper, and he often got into arguments and sometimes brawls. He gambled in card games and on horse races, and he liked to drink. Cummins was a poor role model for a young boy, but he took care of Tom and taught him about life on the farm. By contrast, Tom was mature beyond his years. He was responsible, reserved, and good-natured.

In 1835, Elizabeth Jackson died. Her daughters had already married and moved away. There was no longer a woman at Jackson's Mill to raise young Laura or Tom. Cummins sent Laura to live with her mother's family in Parkersburg, Virginia, where she would be cared for by

Later in life, Tom did not see his sister, Laura Jackson Arnold, as often as he would have liked. The siblings were close, however, and Tom frequently wrote to his "endeared and only Sister."

aunts. Tom was sent to live with another aunt and uncle, Polly and Isaac Brake, near Clarksburg. Brother and sister would never live together again and would see each other only occasionally.

Life on the Brakes' farm was miserable. Isaac Brake made Tom work hard and whipped him as punishment for any minor offense. One day Tom decided to leave the farm and the cruel Brakes behind. He walked the 18 miles (29 km) to Jackson's Mill, where he lived with Cummins for the next seven years.

Tom's life at Jackson's Mill was typical of a boy's life in the rural south in the 1830s. He worked hard on the farm, plowing, helping his uncles cut timber, and hauling the wood by wagon to the sawmill. He hunted wild game, and he fished in the nearby West Fork River. Tom attended several schools near Jackson's Mill and near or in the nearby town of Weston. Classes were generally held in one- or two-room schoolhouses, private homes, or churches. Students learned by memorizing their subjects and reciting their lessons for their teacher. Tom studied reading, writing, spelling, arithmetic, history, and geography.

In his early teens, Tom began to think seriously about religion. At the age of fourteen, he began to study the Bible and to attend services at churches throughout Lewis County. Tom considered becoming a minister, but he decided against it. He thought his education was inadequate, and he was uncomfortable speaking in front of groups. Still, his faith would grow stronger over time.

Throughout his teens, Tom continued to work on Cummins Jackson's farm. When he turned seventeen, Tom, who had by then adopted the middle name Jonathan, was appointed constable of Lewis County. As a constable, Tom was responsible for collecting debts and summoning people to appear before a judge. He was good at his job and won the respect of many people in the area. Not long after his eighteenth birthday, Tom applied for admission to the U.S. Military Academy at West Point, New York. He thought the military might be a good career, and he knew that the education he would receive at West Point would help him in any profession. Cadets were appointed by their state representatives to Congress. Tom approached Virginian congressman Samuel J. Hays and asked to be considered for the post.

The appointment went to another young man, but Tom got a second chance when that cadet abruptly left the academy only days after his arrival. Tom went to Washington, D.C., to see Congressman Hays, taking several letters of support from influential people at home. Hays was surprised to hear that his first appointment had already left West Point, but he thought that Tom might make a good replacement cadet. After passing a difficult entrance examination, Tom was allowed to enroll at the academy. Tom Jackson was about to embark on a new adventure, one that would transform him from a quiet farm boy into a disciplined soldier.

3. A Cadet at West Point

In the summer of 1842, Tom Jackson arrived at West Point. He was a plebe, as first-year cadets at the academy were called. Most people, cadets and professors alike, thought he was shy and odd. Jackson had always been a quiet, even a reclusive, boy. He was tall and strong for his age, but not muscular or athletic. He was awkward on horseback and even on foot. At West Point, he was surrounded by strangers, many of whom were wealthier, more fashionable, and better educated than he was. Jackson knew that he was unprepared for life at West Point, but he was determined to do well.

West Point was built on the banks of the Hudson River about 50 miles (80.5 km) north of New York City. Cadets lived in buildings called barracks. They woke up at sunrise and reported for formal roll call before their rooms and belongings were inspected. They ate breakfast quickly and spent the morning in class. After a brief lunch, they returned to class, then spent the rest of the afternoon marching in formation. After supper, they studied in their rooms until ten o'clock, when they had to be in bed.

The U.S. Military Academy at West Point was founded in 1802, to educate young men and make them professional soldiers. One cadet, who saw Tom Jackson the day he arrived at West Point, noticed the serious expression on Jackson's face and commented, "That fellow looks as if he has come to stay."

Jackson worked very hard throughout his four years at West Point. At night, after all of the candles in the barracks had been put out, he studied by the light of a fire. He had a few friends but rarely went to the parties, dances, and dinners that other cadets enjoyed. The long walks he took along the Hudson River or in the hills nearby were his only breaks from his studies. Classmates called him Old Jack, because he was so quiet and so serious.

Despite his hard work, Jackson had difficulty in every class. When he was called on to recite his lessons or to

As a cadet at the U.S. Military Academy, the ever-serious Tom Jackson earned the nickname Old Jack. Cadets and professors admired Jackson's hard work and discipline. Years later, one of them remembered that "he rose steadily year by year, till we used to say: 'If we had to stay here another year, "old Jack" would be at the head of the class.'" George Horatio Derby, who graduated from West Point in 1846, drew this cadet.

write something on the blackboard, he usually broke out in a sweat, spoke haltingly, and had trouble keeping the chalk from slipping through his fingers. As a plebe, Jackson took algebra, geometry, and trigonometry, which are mathematics courses. During his years at West Point, he also studied French, English grammar, drawing, chemistry, natural philosophy, ethics, mineralogy, engineering, artillery, and cavalry. The material was more advanced than anything he had ever studied, and he struggled to do well. His performance improved each year.

Jackson went home only once while he was a student at West Point. The summer after his second year, he visited his uncle Cummins at Jackson's Mill and his sister Laura, who was living with relatives in Beverly. Soon after Jackson returned to the academy, eighteen-year-old Laura married Jonathan Arnold. Their first son, born three years later, would be named Thomas Jackson for his uncle. Jackson got along well with his new brother-in-law and would be particularly close to his nephew Thomas.

In 1846, Jackson graduated from West Point ranked seventeenth of the fifty-nine cadets in his class. Graduates became brevet, or honorary, second lieutenants in the U.S. Army and were assigned to different branches of the service according to their class rank. The highest-ranking graduates were assigned posts in the engineering corps, the next best became artillerists, the best after that joined the cavalry, and the lowest-ranking graduates became infantrymen. Jackson graduated in the upper third of his class and became a brevet second lieutenant in the 3rd U.S. Artillery. He entered the service just as the nation prepared for war.

Long-brewing tensions between the United States and Mexico had pushed the two countries close to war. Many Americans believed that the United States had a natural right to all the territory west to the Pacific Ocean. Americans were eager to settle the frontier and to exploit its natural resources. By 1846, many settlers had traveled to Texas and beyond, to what are now the states of Oregon and California. Texas had been a Mexican territory until 1836, when it had won a war of independence and had been established as the Republic of Texas. In 1845, Texas had been granted statehood by the U.S. Congress. Mexico had challenged the United States's claims to Texas and to the territory of California. In May 1846, just before Tom Jackson and his classmates graduated from West Point, President James K. Polk had sent American troops under General Zachary Taylor to the Rio Grande, the border between Texas and Mexico. Mexican forces had attacked Taylor north of the river, on American soil, signaling the start of a full-scale war.

Jackson and his classmates anxiously hoped that the war would last long enough for them to test their bravery in battle. Jackson was soon ordered to report to Company K of the 1st U.S. Artillery at Fort Columbus, New York. His military career was about to begin.

4. War in Mexico

Thomas Jackson was anxious to test himself in battle. He arrived at Fort Columbus late in the summer of 1846, only to find that his new unit had already left for Mexico. The company commander, Captain Francis Taylor, had stayed behind at Fort Columbus to recruit men and round up horses for his battery. Within a few weeks, Taylor, Jackson, and the rest of Taylor's command marched to Pittsburgh, Pennsylvania, traveled by ship to New Orleans, Louisiana, and then moved on to Texas. They joined the rest of Company K, stationed in the city of Monterrey, Mexico, in November.

By that time, American troops had won battles at Palo Alto and Resaca de la Palma, occupied Matamoros, and captured Monterrey. Many Americans thought that General Zachary Taylor's little army had already won the war. In truth, Taylor's force was outnumbered nearly five to one, and the Mexican army was not prepared to surrender. A second American army was soon organized in Texas, under General Winfield Scott, to capture the capital at Mexico City and bring the war to a decisive end.

Thomas Jackson, the 1st Artillery, and most of Taylor's force were transferred to Scott's new army, which soon arrived in Mexico. In early 1847, Scott's army landed on the coast at Vera Cruz, reinforced by units which had served under Taylor. Scott's force laid siege to the town. The conflict raged both day and night. After several weeks, the defending troops surrendered. Not long after, Jackson was promoted to the permanent grade of second lieutenant, and Scott's army continued to march inland toward Mexico City.

General Winfield Scott was photographed around 1849 by Mathew Brady. Scott's men called him Old Fuss and Feathers because he was strict about military formalities.

In April, Scott's army skirmished near the mountain town of Cerro Gordo, and in May the Americans reached Puebla, just southeast of Mexico City. With their six- to twelve-month terms of service over, nearly a third of Scott's army left camp to return home. Many of the remaining soldiers were ill from yellow fever and similar diseases. New units arrived throughout the spring and summer, and Scott's army grew larger.

During the summer, Jackson was transferred from one unit to the next as Scott's army was reorganized. Jackson eventually joined Company I of the 1st Artillery. Eager to see combat, he was disappointed to spend the spring and most of the summer as part of the force occupying the Mexican town of Jalapa. Finally, in August, Scott's army started toward Mexico City. The Mexican army was stretched between the towns of Contreras and Churubusco, southwest of Mexico City. On August 19 and 20, 1847, the Americans attacked.

The fighting was fierce, and many American soldiers were killed or wounded. After one of his officers was wounded, Captain John B. Magruder, who commanded Jackson and the rest of Company I, ordered Jackson to take charge of two cannons and direct their fire. The Americans held their position until after dark, then withdrew. They had occupied the enemy's attention long enough for Scott to find a weakness in the Mexican lines. The next day, the Americans attacked from several directions at once. The Mexicans ran away after a short fight, and the Americans chased them to the other end of the defensive line at the town of Churubusco. There the Mexicans put up a stubborn fight. Only after fighting all day did Scott's men force the Mexican army to withdraw.

Opposite: The United States annexed Texas (_red_) in 1845. This angered Mexican officials, because the territory had been part of their country. They were further upset when the United States wanted California (_green_). Diplomatic relations between the countries crumbled, and the Mexican-American War began in the spring of 1846.

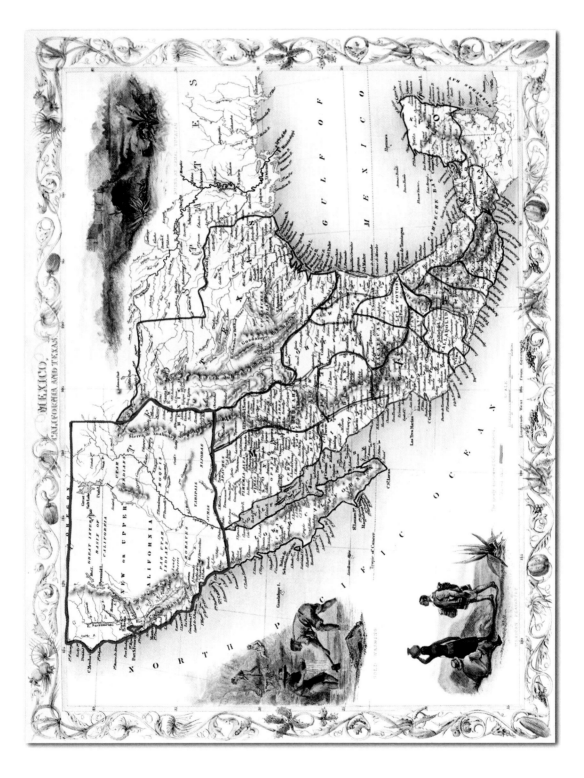

Jackson had finally faced the enemy in a real battle. He had felt a great calmness, and he believed that the excitement of being under fire had made him focus his attention and expertise. His bravery at Contreras earned him two promotions, to the permanent grade of first lieutenant and the brevet grade of captain. On September 8, 1847, the Americans won another battle, at Molino del Rey, a fortified position 2.5 miles (4 km) southwest of Mexico City. Scott's force attacked the Mexican army head-on and suffered many casualties, but the Americans managed to take the position in spite of their losses and were one step closer to the capital city.

Chapultepec, a large fort just east of Molino del Rey, was one of the last defenses guarding the entrance to the Mexican capital. Scott planned to attack the fort from two directions with his infantry and artillery, including Jackson's two-gun section of Magruder's battery. The battle began early on the morning of September 13, 1847. As the guns blasted in every direction, Jackson saw an opportunity and took it. He rushed his cannons close to the fort. Cannonballs and bullets were flying all around him, hitting his men and horses. His soldiers were afraid. Desperate to keep his men in position, Jackson walked back and forth in the road leading up to the fort shouting to his men, "There is no danger! See? I am not hit!" When General William J. Worth ordered Jackson to retreat to safety, the young lieutenant refused, saying it was more dangerous to pull back than to stay in position or advance. A few soldiers helped Jackson to reposition a cannon to fire at the Mexicans, and the small American force stayed in position until infantry reinforcements arrived and charged the fort.

When the Americans attacked, most of the Mexicans ran away, though some fighting continued for the rest of the day. On September 14, 1847, American forces entered Mexico City. Scott's little army had won the war. Jackson's performance at Contreras

This photograph of a twenty-three-year-old Lieutenant Jackson was taken on August 20, 1847. One of the generals praised the "coolness and determination . . . whilst under fire" that Jackson demonstrated while serving in Mexico.

and Chapultepec had played a pivotal role in those victories. Jackson was promoted again, this time to the brevet grade of major, and was personally complimented for his bravery by General Scott.

The war was finished, but negotiations between the United States and Mexico dragged on for months before a treaty was signed in February 1848. Jackson stayed in Mexico until the following summer. He saw the sights, learned local customs, taught himself Spanish, and attended parties and dances. He also visited churches and spoke with priests and monks about the teachings of the Catholic Church. By the summer of 1848, the last of the American troops had left Mexico. Jackson took a ship from Jalapa to New Orleans, arriving back on American soil in July and reporting for duty at Fort Columbus, New York, by August.

He had left for Mexico the summer before as an untested brevet second lieutenant. He returned home as a brevet major who had proven that he was brave and bold. He had learned that a daring general was often a successful one. His career was just beginning, and there seemed to be no limit to what he might accomplish.

5. An Army Officer and a Professor

At Fort Columbus and nearby Fort Hamilton, Thomas Jackson approached his new job as he did everything else: with great care and discipline. He read the regulations, familiarized himself with every aspect of garrison life, and worked hard to fulfill his duties. Jackson did not work all the time, though. He spent time studying military history, especially the campaigns of French general Napoléon Bonaparte. He also spent considerable time worrying about his health. Jackson suffered from a condition called dyspepsia, or a nervous or upset stomach. He wrote long letters to Laura, describing each of his physical complaints and giving her advice on how she could improve her own health. He kept to a strict diet of plain bread and water, maybe with a little meat and a few vegetables or fruits. Jackson also suffered from rheumatism, or swelling and pain in his joints. His rode his horse and did other exercises every day. People often observed Jackson as he walked, pumping or swinging his arms with each stride. Jackson also experimented with the increasingly popular "water

At various times throughout his life, Thomas Jackson suffered from cloudy eyesight, chronic ear infections that resulted in partial deafness, throat inflammations, and, as he explains in this letter to Laura Jackson dated April 1, 1850, "the chill bain," or chilblain, an inflammation of the hands, feet, and ears resulting from exposure to moist, cold weather.

cures," visiting hot springs and bathing in the waters. It is hard to say whether these practices improved Jackson's health, but he had faith in this method, and that certainly improved his spirits.

Jackson also became more interested in Christianity and more devoted to God than ever before. He studied the Bible and prayed every day. He examined his faith with the help of ministers and religious-minded friends, especially his commander, Captain Francis Taylor. He mentioned his faith in almost every letter that he wrote to Laura. His sister, troubled by her own poor health and the illness of a daughter, turned away from Christianity at about the same time that her brother embraced it. "I told you I believed that God would restore me to perfect health, and such continues to be my belief," he wrote her in the spring of 1850, reminding her that "my daily prayers are for your salvation."

In the fall of that year, Jackson was transferred to Company E of the 1st Artillery, commanded by Captain William E. French. Jackson's new company was soon transferred to Fort Meade, near Tampa, Florida. French and Jackson got along at first, but that soon changed. Jackson, as company quartermaster, was responsible for directing the construction of new buildings at Fort Meade. French, as company commander, suggested changes to Jackson's plans, which Jackson resented. Soon the two men spoke only while on duty, and eventually each made a formal complaint against the other. Their superior officer ruled that Jackson must obey his commander's orders. Jackson, bored by his duties and frustrated by his dispute with French, was convinced that he would not be promoted for many months or even years. Fortunately, he was unexpectedly offered a position elsewhere.

In the spring of 1851, Colonel Francis H. Smith, superintendent of the Virginia Military Institute in Lexington, Virginia, wrote to Jackson and offered him a teaching position at the institute. The professorship was in the department of natural philosophy, an area of study like modern physics. Jackson had no expertise in this subject and no experience as a teacher, but he was considered an ideal candidate. Not only was he a West Point graduate and a hero of the Mexican War, but he was also a Virginian. Jackson promptly accepted the job. He visited Lexington for the first time in June, met professors and cadets, and toured the institute campus.

Cadets, such as this one, at VMI even wore their uniforms to class. Cadets under Jackson's instruction sometimes made fun of his rigidity and his dullness as a professor.

Of his appointment to the faculty of the Virginia Military Institute, Jackson wrote to his sister, "I consider the position both conspicuous and desirable." The institute was founded in 1839, and was the first of several southern military academies modeled on the U.S. Military Academy at West Point. Often referred to by its initials, VMI, it has also been called the West Point of the South. In 1857, Casimir Bohn made this hand-colored engraving of Lexington, with the castlelike buildings of the institute to the right.

Jackson did not know whether or not he would make a good professor, but he believed that God had given him the opportunity to find out, and he was determined to do his best.

The Virginia Military Institute was sponsored by the state of Virginia and offered an advanced education. Its purpose was to educate young men in mathematics, the sciences, and engineering to prepare them for any civilian career and to give them basic military training to prepare them for service in state or federal forces. The schedule for cadets and professors was much like that at West Point. Jackson read and memorized material late into the night to prepare for the next day's lectures. His cadets were expected to take detailed notes and to memorize almost everything he said. In class they were asked to recite, or to stand at attention, salute, and answer any question he asked them. Jackson would also summon them to the blackboard to solve scientific or mathematical problems.

Major Jackson was a terribly dull professor. As Colonel Smith remembered many years later, "He was no teacher. . . .He was a brave man, a conscientious man, and a good man, but he was no professor." Jackson never showed any enthusiasm for his lectures. For Jackson, as for his cadets, his lectures were simply something to endure. The most capable cadets did well, and cadets of average intelligence learned if they concentrated hard enough. Cadets with the least aptitude for natural and experimental philosophy struggled and failed. They needed additional help, but they never got it from Jackson. He treated every student exactly the same way.

Jackson knew quite well that he had many limitations as a professor, but he persevered. As he settled into the routine at VMI, he began to appreciate his colleagues there and the picturesque Shenandoah Valley countryside nearby. "Things promise well," Jackson wrote to Laura in the fall of 1852, at the end of his first year in Lexington. "Of all places which have come under my observation in the United States, this little village is the most beautiful."

Of the people he met in Lexington, he wrote to Laura, "I admire the citizens of this place very much." However, his eccentric behavior and awkward manners made him an easy target for gossip and criticism in the small town. If a colleague or a friend included the casual phrase "You know" in conversation, Jackson would answer without smiling, "No, I don't know." At dinners and parties, Jackson approached everything, even conversation, as if it were his duty to be nice, but he often declined the food being served because it was not part of his strict diet.

In the mid-1800s, Lexington, Virginia, was a small town in the Shenandoah Valley. This photograph shows North Main Street around 1867. VMI is visible in the distance.

Eager to join a religious community, Jackson visited all the churches in town. Some of his closest friends in Lexington were Presbyterians. They invited Jackson to go to services at Lexington Presbyterian Church with them and to learn about their denomination. Jackson soon joined the church and became one of its most enthusiastic and faithful members, eventually serving as chairman of the deacons, or church officers.

At church, Jackson met and made friends, who came to accept and admire his eccentricities. His good friends John Lyle and Harvey and Isabella Hill were members of Lexington Presbyterian Church. Friend George Junkin was the president of nearby Washington College and a Presbyterian minister. He and Jackson talked often about religion, education, and other topics. Dr. Junkin and his wife, Julia, had two daughters. The younger, Elinor, or Ellie, was a year younger than Jackson. It did not take long for the two to become friends, and, by the end of 1852, much more. "I don't know what has changed me," Jackson complained to Harvey Hill. Hill laughed and responded, "You are in love; that's what is the matter!"

On August 4, 1853, Thomas Jackson and Ellie Junkin were married. He was twenty-nine years old, and she was twenty-eight years old. They took a long honeymoon through the Northeast and Canada, arriving back in Lexington in time for the new school year. Major Thomas Jackson was a changed man. People in town said that he was happier than anybody had ever seen him. He and Ellie lived with the Junkins, and Jackson belonged to a large and loving family for the first time. That winter the couple discovered that they were going to have a baby.

Soon tragedy struck. In the mid-nineteenth century, childbirth was dangerous for mothers and babies alike. Babies were usually born at home, not in hospitals. Few doctors specialized in birthing, and the dangers of infection were not widely known or under-

Several months after his wife's death, Thomas Jackson wrote, "I cannot realize that Ellie is gone; that my wife will no more cheer the rugged and dark way of life."

stood. On October 22, 1854, Ellie gave birth to a little boy. The baby was stillborn, or born dead. Ellie became quite ill and died within an hour.

Jackson was overwhelmed by the tragedy. He had lost not only a son, but his new wife, too. He visited his wife's grave every day and sometimes said that he wanted to die. He was comforted only by the belief that Ellie and the baby were in heaven and that everything happened according to God's plan. He tried to concentrate on his classes at VMI and on services and prayer meetings at church, but his family and friends worried that he might never recover from Ellie's death.

When Jackson returned to Lexington for the beginning of the next school year, he decided to organize a Sunday school class at the Presbyterian Church for the slaves and free blacks who lived in and near Lexington. The group, led by Jackson, met on Sunday afternoons and heard prayers, sang hymns, and studied Bible verses. Jackson believed that blacks should have the same opportunity as whites to learn about God. This was a controversial opinion. Many white people thought it was dangerous to teach blacks to read, write, or interpret the Bible. The Bible tells of enslaved people who, through the strength of their faith, win their freedom. Slave owners feared that slaves and free blacks who read the Bible might be influenced to work, and perhaps even to fight, for freedom and equality. Many white southerners, including Thomas Jackson, believed that God approved of slavery. They argued that slaves were housed, clothed, and fed better in the American South than elsewhere. Moreover, they claimed that in America slaves were introduced to Christianity and benefited from its "civilizing" influences. There was a growing movement in America, however, that called for an end to the institution of slavery. Members of this movement were called abolitionists.

In the summer of 1856, Jackson decided to take a three-month vacation in Europe. Jackson visited most

Of his efforts to establish and maintain a Sunday school for blacks, one of Thomas Jackson's friends wrote that Jackson "threw himself into this work with all of his characteristic energy and wisdom." Other Lexington residents were not as enthusiastic about the school. Some accounts from the time claim that Jackson was widely criticized and even threatened with prosecution.
H. B. Hull took this 1855 daguerreotype of Jackson.

of the great cities of Europe, including London, Rome, and Paris, and traveled throughout England, Scotland, Belgium, Germany, Switzerland, Italy, and France. He took pages of notes, and when he returned to Lexington, Jackson wrote to Laura that to describe everywhere he had gone and everything he had seen on his trip, he would have to write a book several hundred pages long or spend several hours telling her stories about his travels.

Jackson's trip gave him time to reflect. He was thirty-two years old, and he was lonely without Ellie, who had been dead for almost two years. Jackson hoped to find a companion with whom he might share his life, and he knew a young lady who might be just the right person.

Mary Anna Morrison, Jackson's second wife, was twenty-five years old at the time of their wedding, seven years younger than her husband. She was known for her sunny disposition.

Her name was Mary Anna Morrison, and friends and family called her Anna. She lived near Charlotte, North Carolina. Jackson and Anna had met three years earlier, when

Anna and her sister Eugenia had traveled to Lexington to visit their sister Isabella Hill. The group had become fast friends. Jackson remembered Anna fondly. He wrote her a letter, saying he hoped they could renew their friendship, then surprised her family a few months later when he arrived at the Morrisons' North Carolina home to see Anna on his Christmas vacation. They enjoyed their time together. The rest of Anna's family liked Jackson very much, too. By the time Jackson returned to VMI, he and Anna were engaged. On July 16, 1857, after a courtship of six months, they were married. They went on a honeymoon to Richmond, Baltimore, and Philadelphia, and then on to New York City, West Point, Niagara Falls, and Saratoga. They spent the last weeks of their trip in Virginia, at the Rockbridge Alum Springs, a hot springs and spa in the mountains near the Shenandoah Valley.

The Jacksons rented a room in the Lexington Hotel, where Jackson had been living for most of the past year. They soon learned that they were going to have a baby, due in the spring of 1858. The couple began to look for a house of their own. In the meantime, they moved into a boardinghouse, or apartment, where they enjoyed a little more privacy.

Anna's baby, whom they named Mary Graham for Anna's mother, was born on April 30, 1858. Within days, Mary got sick. She died on May 25. Jackson and Anna were crushed by their grief, but they were comforted by

Thomas Jackson purchased this Washington Street house on November 4, 1858, for $3,000, which is equivalent to about $55,000 today. The large, old house was in need of many repairs, and Jackson enthusiastically undertook these projects, eager to transform his first house into a comfortable home.

their faith and by the arrival of Jackson's thirteen-year-old nephew, Thomas Jackson Arnold, who came to Lexington that fall to live with his uncle and aunt. The Jacksons bought a house soon after, and the three moved into the two-story brick house early in 1859. It stood on Washington Street, a short walk from VMI and the Lexington Presbyterian Church. "He was intensely fond of his home, and it was there he found his greatest happiness," Anna said of her husband years later.

6. The Divided Union, a Civil War, and a New Name

As the 1850s ended, disagreements between the North and the South over slavery threatened to split the country in two. Proslavery and antislavery factions debated the issue in newspapers, in public meetings, on street corners, and in sometimes violent protests. John Brown was one of the most outspoken abolitionists engaged in the public debate over slavery. On October 16, 1859, Brown and several men, armed with guns and swords, captured the undefended U.S. arsenal at Harpers Ferry, in modern-day West Virginia. They hoped to steal the weapons stored there and start a slave rebellion that would spread across the South. Brown was captured and put on trial for treason and for trying to start a slave rebellion. He pleaded guilty, was convicted, and was hanged on December 2, 1859. Virginia Military Institute cadets, under the command of several professors, including Major Jackson, were ordered to witness Brown's execution.

In 1860, the country held a presidential election. The race was a battle between the Republicans, who

This sketch by Albert Berghaus shows John Brown being led to his execution. Jackson wrote a long letter to his wife, Anna, describing the execution of John Brown. "He behaved with unflinching firmness," Jackson wrote with some admiration. "It was an imposing but very solemn scene." Jackson prayed for Brown's soul, explaining, "I hope that he was prepared to die, but I am doubtful."

were opposed to slavery, and the Democrats, who were divided on the issue. Northern Democrats were opposed to the expansion of slavery into new territories and states but not to its continued existence in the South. Southern Democrats were in favor of expanding slavery into any new territories and states. Each Democratic faction nominated a candidate for president, dividing the party's vote and ruining any hope for victory. The Republican Party nominated Abraham Lincoln. He opposed slavery and its expansion into new territories. He believed, however, that as long as the law allowed slavery in any part of the country, the law should be obeyed and the union of states preserved at all costs.

Democrats feared that if Lincoln won the election the federal government would seek to abolish slavery. Many argued that the southern states should secede from the United States. They believed that the only way they could protect their rights, including the right to own slaves, was to form a new country. Lincoln was elected president on

In his inauguration speech, Abraham Lincoln asked Americans to consider the crisis before them. "We are not enemies, but friends," he said. "We must not be enemies." Alexander Hesler photographed Lincoln in 1860.

November 6, 1860, and the South did not wait long to act. In December, South Carolina became the first state to secede. Mississippi, Florida, Alabama, Georgia, Louisiana, and Texas seceded in January and February 1861. These states organized a centralized government as the Confederate States of America and elected Jefferson Davis as their first president.

The threat of war loomed. Several southern states, in preparation for war, had already taken possession of

On April 14, 1861, after thirty-four hours of bombardment, the defeated Union soldiers surrendered and evacuated Fort Sumter, and the victorious Confederates raised their flag above the parade ground, shown here in a photograph taken in the days just after the Union defeat. Confederate forces would occupy the fort until February 1865.

U.S. forts and other federal property. One of the most important forts still in federal hands was Fort Sumter, at Charleston, South Carolina. When the Confederates told the federal soldiers stationed in the fort to surrender, the Federals refused. On April 12, 1861, the Confederates fired their cannons at Fort Sumter, and the Federals in the fort fired back. After a day and a half, the Federal soldiers surrendered the fort. The Civil War had begun. In April and May, Virginia, Arkansas, Tennessee, and North Carolina seceded and joined the Confederacy.

Jackson truly loved the Union, but he loved Virginia more and pledged his loyalty to the Confederate States.

The war would separate Jackson and his sister, Laura, forever. As were most western Virginians, Laura was a strong Unionist. Western Virginia, including Jackson's Mill and the surrounding countryside, would remain loyal to the Union and would become the new state of West Virginia in 1863. After the outbreak of war, Laura and Jackson never saw or wrote to each other again.

Jackson was ordered to take the entire corps of cadets from the Virginia Military Institute to the state capital at Richmond. He left Anna, VMI, and Lexington on April 21. He would never see his house or his adopted hometown again. Within a week, Jackson was appointed a colonel of the Virginia state forces and was assigned to take charge of the units being assembled at Harpers Ferry, a strategic point on the Potomac River. Jackson and his officers drilled their men diligently, turning volunteers into soldiers. Confederate general Joseph E. Johnston arrived in May and took command, impressed by what Jackson had accomplished in such a short time. Johnston gave Jackson command of a brigade and recommended his promotion to brigadier general in the Confederate army, which became effective in June.

Jackson's First Virginia Brigade was made of the 2nd, 4th, 5th, 27th, and 33rd Virginia infantry regiments and the Rockbridge Artillery. Many of the soldiers were natives of the Shenandoah Valley. They had been farmers, doctors, lawyers, bankers, businessmen, clerks, or college students before the war began. Most ranged in age from

The Union and Confederate armies were organized into small fighting forces that could be commanded individually or in groups. A company, commanded by a captain, included about one hundred men. Ten companies formed a regiment, such as the 4th Virginia Infantry, commanded by a colonel. Three to five regiments formed a brigade, commanded by a brigadier general or sometimes a colonel. Two to four brigades formed a division, commanded by a brigadier general or a major general. Two to three divisions formed a corps, commanded by a major general or sometimes a lieutenant general in the Confederate army. Several corps formed an army, commanded by a major general in the U.S. Army or a general in the Confederate army.

eighteen to twenty-five years old. They had answered the call to arms with enthusiasm and optimism. They, like their northern counterparts, thought that a single, large battle would bring a speedy conclusion to the war with minimal bloodshed. They were horribly wrong.

Almost 250,000 American soldiers were killed in battle or died of wounds in the Civil War, making it the deadliest war Americans had fought up to that time. Tactics had not changed greatly in fifty years, but advances in the design and production of weapons had made war much more deadly. Infantrymen, or foot soldiers, were the most common soldiers. They generally fought in lines side by side and two rows deep.

The Model 1861 Springfield rifle and the British Pattern 1853 Enfield rifle, which is shown here, were the most common firearms used by Union and Confederate infantrymen during the Civil War. Both rifles were well made and accurate, and they fired the most common Civil War bullet, the minié ball. The minié ball was named for its inventor, Frenchman Claude Minié. It was a hollow, cone-shaped, .58- or .577-caliber lead bullet, measuring about 1 inch (2.5 cm) end to end and .5 inch (1.3 cm) across at the base.

Opposing lines marched to within 500 yards (457.2 m) of each other and sometimes as close as 50 yards (45.7 m), and fired their guns. Their rifles, which weighed about 9 pounds (4.1 kg) and were about 5 feet (1.5 m) long, had an effective range of about 250 yards (228.6 m). Units defending a position often sought protection in trenches or behind earthworks or log breastworks. Cavalrymen, traveling and fighting on horseback, were most often used to scout an enemy's position or to make raids against enemy supply lines. They were armed with pistols, carbines or repeaters, and swords. Artillerymen moved, loaded, and fired cannons in batteries, or groups of two to six cannons.

Most Civil War soldiers wore woolen uniforms. Some wore cotton. Though Union soldiers usually wore dark

Union uniforms, such as the one on the left, were issued by the U.S. government. They stayed relatively unchanged throughout the Civil War. Confederate uniforms, such as the one on the right, often came from different sources. Soldiers sometimes had to replace pieces of their uniforms by taking them from the dead. As a result, Confederate uniforms looked increasingly varied, shabby, and ill-fitting as the war progressed.

blue and Confederate soldiers usually wore gray, uniforms were different from unit to unit and designs changed over time. Soldiers wore cotton or wool socks, simple leather shoes called brogans, and a cap or hat. Union soldiers preferred the kepi, a dark blue wool cap with a sloped crown and a leather visor. Confederate soldiers preferred the slouch hat, a dark, wide-brimmed, felt hat. Soldiers carried their belongings, usually a tin cup, a fork or spoon, writing paper, and pens or pencils, in a backpack or rolled up in a blanket slung across their shoulders. They also carried a tin canteen and sometimes a cartridge box, or a leather pouch that held their bullets.

Union and Confederate soldiers, known as Yankees and Rebels respectively, were promised rations every day, but they often went without, especially on the march or in battle. Each soldier was allowed about 1 pound (.5 kg) of meat, often bacon or salt-cured pork, and 1 pound of bread per day. Soldiers also received peas, beans, rice, sugar, salt, and coffee when it was available. They often ate hardtack, or thick crackers, which was easy to carry and did not spoil quickly. Soldiers also foraged for food, buying or sometimes stealing what they wanted from civilians.

In the summer of 1861, General Irvin McDowell commanded the main Federal army defending the Union capital of

General Irvin McDowell was photographed at the Mathew Brady Studio between 1860 and 1865.

Washington, D.C. McDowell's forces faced the Army of the Potomac, the main Confederate army in Virginia, which was commanded by General P.G.T. Beauregard. Beauregard's army guarded Manassas Junction, a strategic rail stop about 30 miles (48.3 km) southwest of Washington, D.C. Joseph E. Johnston's Confederate Army of the Shenandoah included Jackson's First Virginia Brigade and was nearby. Most of Johnston's men joined Beauregard on July 20, and Johnston took command of the combined force.

In the early morning of July 21, 1861, McDowell's and Johnston's armies met just north of Manassas Junction. The Federals, who slightly outnumbered the Confederates, were initially successful, pushing the Confederates from their original position to a hill overlooking a creek called Bull Run. Around

During the Mexican War, West Point graduate Barnard Elliott Bee was wounded and was promoted three times. He became a Confederate general in the summer of 1861, and was badly wounded in his first battle, at Bull Run. He died the next day. This sketch was made from life by Conrad Chapman.

noon, General Barnard E. Bee, whose brigade was one of several Confederate units holding their ground under great pressure, noticed Jackson's brigade nearby. The brigade had been under heavy cannon fire for some time. Several of Jackson's men had been killed or wounded. Jackson himself had been wounded in the hand by a piece of a cannonball, but he refused to leave the battlefield to see a surgeon. Bee, hoping to encourage his men, pointed to Jackson's Virginians and

Attached to a tree on the battlefield at Bull Run is a plaque that reads, "Here Jackson was wounded and got the title of Stone Wall, July 21, 1861."

exclaimed, "Look, men, there is Jackson standing like a stone wall!" General Bee's exclamation gave Jackson and his brigade one of the most famous nicknames in American history. Barnard E. Bee was wounded later that day on the battlefield and died the next day.

Throughout the long day, Jackson's brigade helped the Confederates to hold their position until reinforcements came. When fresh units arrived late in the afternoon, Johnston ordered an attack along the entire line, forcing McDowell northeast. The Federals withdrew slowly at first, then panicked and ran. The Rebels

The Battle of Bull Run was a shocking start to the war. Northerners realized that the war to preserve the Union would be longer and bloodier than they had expected. By contrast, Southerners rejoiced, believing that the war was finished or would end soon. In this photograph by George N. Barnard, members of the Federal cavalry gather across the river from a group of Confederate children, after the battle.

pursued briefly but were almost as disorganized in their victory as the Yankees were in their defeat. This battle was called Bull Run by Northerners, who named it for the creek, and Manassas by Southerners, who named it for the railroad junction nearby.

Thomas Jackson was a hero of the battle. Southern newspapers repeated the account of Bee's rousing cheer. The Stonewall Brigade would become one of the most famous units in the Confederate army. Not long before he died, Jackson would say, "The men of that brigade will be some day proud to say to their children, 'I was one of the Stonewall brigade.'"

In the months following the Battle of Manassas, the capital of the Confederacy moved from Montgomery, Alabama, to Richmond, Virginia, about 90 miles (144.8 km) south of Washington, D.C. In October, Jackson was promoted again, this time to major general, and was given command of all the Confederate forces in the Shenandoah Valley. His army, numbering about four thousand men by November, was called the Army of the Shenandoah and sometimes the Army of the Valley. Its headquarters was at the strategically important town of Winchester, near the northern end of the valley and about 60 miles (96.6 km) northwest of Washington, D.C.

The Shenandoah Valley stood between Washington, D.C., and Richmond. It could serve as the staging ground for either army's attack on its enemy's capital. Jackson knew that holding Winchester was crucial if the Confederates were to maintain control of the valley and prevent a Federal advance on Richmond. Jackson believed that Federal troops in and around Romney, about 25 miles (40.2 km) northwest of Winchester, presented a threat to his force, and he decided to send a portion of his army on an expedition there. On January 1, 1862, Jackson and his men, accompanied by three brigades commanded by General William W. Loring, left Winchester bound for Romney. It was a hard march over

The Shenandoah Valley is bounded by the Allegheny Mountains to the west and the Blue Ridge Mountains to the east. It stretches more than 120 miles (193.1 km) southwest from the Potomac River to Lexington, Virginia. In the 1860s, the valley was a patchwork of farms that produced wheat, corn, cows, pigs, milk, butter, leather, and wool. It fed, clothed, and supplied many Confederate soldiers and southern civilians.

mountainous terrain in snow and ice, and many soldiers got sick on the way. Loring and other officers challenged Jackson's course of action, but Jackson persevered. After a two-week march, Jackson's men arrived in Romney to find that the Federals had recently evacuated the town. The campaign had accomplished very little but to demonstrate Jackson's single-minded devotion to duty and his insistence that his officers obey his orders whether or not they agreed with or even understood them.

Stonewall Jackson and his men spent two more months in camp at Winchester, waiting for the chance to fight the Federals. When it came, they would make the most of it. He and his soldiers would become famous.

7. "Oh, for a Dozen Jacksons!"

Things were not going well for the South in the spring of 1862. Federal troops occupied large areas throughout the Confederacy. Southern civilians watched anxiously, and some abandoned their homes, as Union armies invaded. Confederate president Jefferson Davis, General Joseph E. Johnston, and Davis's military advisor, Robert E. Lee, knew that Union general George B. McClellan was stationed on the Virginian peninsula east of Richmond, organizing and training a huge Federal army, called the Army of the Potomac, to attack the capital. The Confederate authorities wanted to prevent additional Union troops from joining McClellan's force and hoped to keep the Shenandoah Valley under

As were many famous Union and Confederate generals, General George Brinton McClellan was a West Point graduate and a veteran of the Mexican War. He is shown here in a photograph by Frederick Gutekunst.

LLOYD'S NEW WAR MAP OF VIRGINIA.

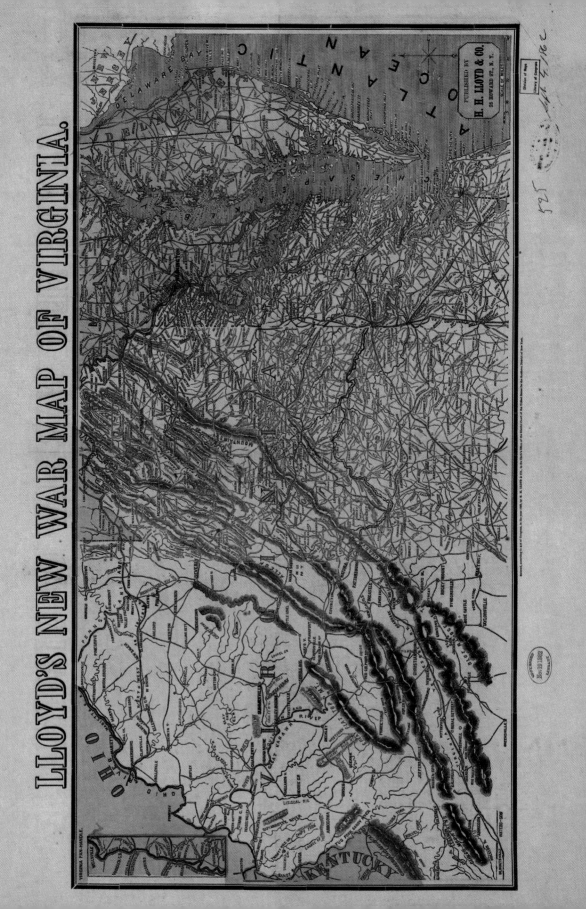

Confederate control. They believed that Jackson's Army of the Valley might be able to do both things, and gave Jackson full responsibility and authority to plan operations in the Shenandoah Valley.

Jackson's first concern was a Federal army commanded by General Nathaniel P. Banks. Banks's force, which was part of the Union Department of the Shenandoah, was more than three times larger than the Confederacy's Army of the Shenandoah. Banks planned to add his men to those of General James Shields and to take the combined troops to McClellan. Jackson knew that he could not allow the Federals to leave the Shenandoah Valley without a fight. On March 23, 1862, he sent the Army of the Valley to Kernstown, a little town just 3 miles (4.8 km) south of Winchester, where Shields was encamped. Jackson, who had little reliable information about the enemy he faced, thought his Rebels outnumbered the Federals and that he could defeat them quickly. He was wrong on both counts. Shields's army was twice as large as Jackson's and defended a strong position on high ground west of the town. After about ninety minutes of fighting, in which neither side gained a clear advantage, Shields sent reinforcements against Jackson's lines. The Confederates held their position as long as they could. Even Jackson's old Stonewall Brigade, under General

---

Opposite: Lloyd's New War Map of Virginia, created in 1862, shows the towns, railroads, and rivers of Virginia, as well as the fields of battle, underlined in red, from the first year of the war.

Richard B. Garnett's command, was forced to withdraw. The Rebels retreated south, away from Kernstown and toward Woodstock, a town 26 miles (41.8 km) away.

Jackson had been defeated, but his tactics and the strength of his force had made a big impression on Shields and Banks. After this battle, Jackson received reinforcements, increasing his strength to more than nine thousand men, and planned his next move. Federal armies were closing in on Jackson. McClellan's army had begun to make its way toward Richmond, and Federal armies had captured Nashville, Tennessee, and New Orleans, Louisiana. People across the Confederacy pinned their hopes on Jackson and his army. "They are the right men in the right place," a columnist for one Richmond newspaper observed.

Jackson's strategy was to attack the various Union armies in the valley with as many men as he could muster. A small Union force under General Robert Milroy was camped near the town of McDowell, near the southern end of the Shenandoah Valley, and Jackson planned an attack. Milroy was ready to meet the Confederate advance. On the morning of May 8, 1862, equipped with only a portion of his total army, Milroy attacked Jackson. The Confederates, who outnumbered the Federals, defended their position stubbornly. Early the next morning, Milroy retreated, acknowledging that he could not force Jackson from the battlefield and giving the Confederates a narrow victory. The Battle of McDowell convinced Nathaniel P. Banks and John C. Frémont, the Union generals in the Shenandoah, that Jackson's army was larger and more dangerous than ever. In truth, the Federal forces had twice as many men and were in position to attack Jackson from more than one direction.

When Confederate general Richard S. Ewell's division joined Jackson in the middle of May, the Army of the Valley grew to seventeen thousand soldiers. Jackson decided to attack a small Federal force stationed at Front Royal, 17 miles (27.4 km) south of Winchester, then move against Banks's main force,

General Richard Stoddart Ewell was Jackson's most trusted subordinate officer. Ewell, who had a high-pitched voice and a strange sense of humor, was one of the more colorful personalities of the war.

encamped at Strasburg, about 10 miles (16.1 km) west of Front Royal. On May 23, 1862, Jackson's Confederates, with Ewell in the lead, pushed the Federals north through Front Royal. Jackson's cavalry and Ewell's infantry charged the Union troops at once, bringing a swift end to the battle. The Federals retreated toward Strasburg. They lost seven hundred men, most of whom were taken prisoner. The Confederates lost very few men. Fewer than one hundred were killed or wounded.

The first part of Jackson's plan had worked. He predicted that Banks would retreat from Strasburg northeast to Winchester as soon as he learned of the battle at Front Royal. Jackson decided to move on Winchester, hoping to arrive before Banks. On May 24, the Army of the Valley marched more than 20 miles (32.2 km) on the winding road north toward Winchester. Jackson knew that he had no time to waste. The two armies were racing to the strategic town. Jackson pushed his soldiers almost all night, refusing to let them stop to rest or eat. Some Confederates later said that they were so tired that they actually slept while they marched. In a letter home, one

The First Battle of Winchester was an important fight. The town was so strategically important, and fighting around it was so common, that it changed hands between Union and Confederate forces seventy-six times during the war. This pencil drawing was made by Edwin Forbes.

captain wrote, ". . . wee have suffered a great deal for the want of sleep and rest [and have] been on forced marches all the time." Most of Jackson's army reached Winchester in the middle of the night, only to learn that Banks had reached the town two hours ahead of the weary Confederate forces.

Just after sunrise on May 25, Jackson sent his army, with the Stonewall Brigade in the lead, against Banks's force. The Federals had taken a strong defensive position on the hills west of the town. Banks's cannons bombarded Jackson's advancing lines. Jackson's cannons stopped in the field to fire back, and neither side gained an advantage. After almost two hours of battle, Jackson ordered most of his men to charge against Banks's defensive lines. Jackson was so excited that he waved his cap and yelled, "Let's holler!" The Confederates ran forward, screaming the rebel yell of "Woh-who-ey! who-ey! who-ey!" with all their might. The Rebel charge broke through the Yankee lines, and most of Banks's army ran away in confusion. The Union soldiers retreated along the Valley Pike toward Martinsburg, about 20 miles (32.2 km) northeast. That day the Federal army had lost about 2,500 men, most of them taken prisoner. The Confederates had lost only about 300 men, most of them killed or wounded.

Southerners and Northerners alike predicted that Jackson would attack Washington, D.C. "Jackson will certainly *make believe* he is after Washington—if indeed he is not really after it," one of his officers claimed in a letter home in May 1862. Jackson's strategy was to mislead the Federals in just this way. Jackson knew that his army was too small to attack the Union capital. However, he knew that if Lincoln believed Jackson might threaten the city, the Confederate army would have a real advantage. Union troops would be sent to defend their capital, leaving fewer soldiers to fight elsewhere.

Union authorities soon ordered additional troops into the Shenandoah Valley. By May 30, Jackson was encamped near Harpers Ferry, hoping to make Federal military and civilian authorities believe he might advance into Maryland. Within days, he learned that two Federal armies, one commanded by Frémont and the other by Shields, were near Strasburg and Front Royal, respectively. If Frémont's fifteen thousand men and Shields's ten thousand men joined forces, their combined army would be about twice as large as Jackson's, which numbered less than thirteen thousand men. Jackson could not risk his troops' safety by waiting for his enemies to catch him.

On May 30 and 31, Jackson retreated to Winchester and then to Strasburg, hoping to find Frémont's army there before it joined with Shields's force. Union forces made no move against Jackson's army at Strasburg, but soon began pursuing him south. Jackson's men marched to New Market, about 25 miles (40.2 km) southeast of Strasburg, arriving just ahead of the

Federals on June 4. Jackson decided that the town of Port Republic, 25 miles (40.2 km) farther southeast, would be the best place for him to stop his retreat and to attempt to defeat each Federal army separately.

By the first week in June, Jackson had divided his army between Port Republic and the nearby town of Cross Keys 5 miles (8 km) north. Jackson planned to lure Frémont, who was following close behind, into attacking the Confederates at Cross Keys before Shields arrived.

On June 8, 1862, portions of Shields's and Jackson's armies skirmished in Port Republic. Meanwhile, at Cross Keys, General Richard S. Ewell's division held a defensive position against Frémont's

This watercolor sketch of the Battle of Cross Keys was made by Private Henry Berckhoff of the Union army. Some 17,000 Union and Confederate soldiers met on the field at Cross Keys, and more than 950 men died.

entire army. The Federals outnumbered the Confederates by more than two to one, but when Frémont attacked Ewell, the Rebels held their ground and even launched a counterattack late in the day, pushing the Yankees a short distance from the battle-field. The Federals lost 684 men, and the Confederates lost 288 men. When Jackson arrived in person at Cross Keys, he was pleased to discover that Ewell had bought valuable time for the Army of the Valley until more Confederate troops could be mustered.

On June 9, Jackson turned his attention to Shields, whose army remained at Port Republic. Jackson ordered Ewell's division to march from Cross Keys to join Jackson in an attack against Shields. Ewell did so, and the Confederates outnumbered the Federals there by more than two to one. The battle began early that morning and developed slowly. The Yankees held their ground against several Rebel attacks, but, by midmorn-ing, Jackson's troops had captured several of Shields's cannons and had pushed the Union infantry into full retreat. The Federals had lost 1,100 men, half of whom were taken prisoner. The Confederates had lost 800 men, many of whom were killed.

After the Battles of Cross Keys and Port Republic, Frémont and Shields, who were surprised by Jackson's aggressive tactics, quickly withdrew their armies from the valley. The Shenandoah Valley campaign was fin-ished. It was one of the greatest triumphs in American military history. Against all odds, Jackson had accomplished what he had set out to do. He had defended the valley from the Federal armies operating there and had prevented Federal reinforcements from joining McClellan near Richmond. Throughout the campaign, Jackson had never commanded more than 17,000 men at any one time, and he had faced several armies with a combined total of as many as 64,000 troops. Jackson's campaign had cost the Union army about 5,400 men, but it had cost the vastly outnumbered Confederates just 2,700 men. Satisfied that the Yankees were leaving, Jackson began to make plans to go to Richmond and join Robert E. Lee. Lee had recently taken command of the main Confederate army in Virginia, which had been renamed the Army of Northern Virginia.

Jackson's Shenandoah Valley campaign made him the most popular general in the Confederacy at a time when many Southerners believed that the Confederate war effort was a failure. His men were proud of him and of themselves. In a letter to his mother, a Confederate artillerist described how the Army of the Valley reacted when Jackson rode by on horseback one day: "I heard at a distance down the road loud cheering. We immediately exclaimed—'Old Jack's coming'—for we knew no one else elicited such shouts—and ran to the road side. . . . As he came on the men pressed in shoals to the road side and waved their hats and cheered enthusiastically. . . . I never saw a more thrilling scene, nor one that

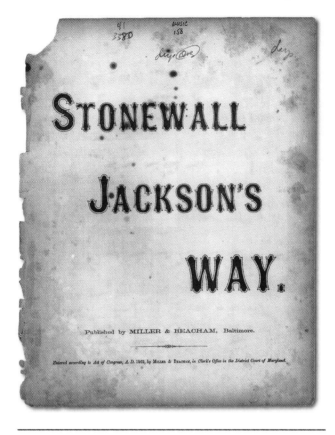

The Shenandoah Valley campaign was celebrated throughout the South in articles, poems, and songs. John Williamson Palmer's popular poem "Stonewall Jackson's Way" was put to music in 1862. The poem warned, "The foe had better ne'er been born/That gets in Stonewall's way!" This sheet music for voice and piano was published in Baltimore, Maryland, by Miller & Beacham.

filled me with more interest." Jackson's victories were celebrated in poems and songs. Newspapers across the South sang his praises. The Charleston *Mercury* said, "A Southern army has, at last, found a fighting leader. . . . Stonewall Jackson has shown himself a true General." The Richmond *Whig* called the Army of the Valley "the pride of the South and the terror of the North. . . . Oh, for a dozen Jacksons!"

8. "One of the Greatest Men Living"

As the summer of 1862 began, Stonewall Jackson and his soldiers went to Richmond, taking with them the hopes of the South. They became part of the Army of Northern Virginia, commanded by Robert E. Lee. Once Jackson's troops arrived, Lee's army numbered almost 90,000 men. The Federal Army of the Potomac, commanded by General George B. McClellan, numbered about 100,000 men. The Army of the Potomac was encamped along a line that was, at its closest, 5 miles (8 km) east of Richmond. The Federal line was divided in two by the Chickahominy River, which created a weak point in their defenses. Lee planned an attack on this weak point. The Federals prepared to attack the Confederates as well.

The campaign, which would come to be known as the Seven Days' Battles, began on June 25, 1862. McClellan advanced on the Confederate lines 5 miles (8 km) east of Richmond. Troops skirmished at White Oak Swamp, but the Federals failed to force the Confederates out of their defensive position. Upon learning that Lee was being reinforced by additional soldiers, McClellan did

When the Civil War began, Abraham Lincoln offered Robert Edward Lee
command of all the Union armies. Loyal to his home state of Virginia,
Lee refused and resigned from the U.S. Army. He was made a general in
the Confederate army and, in June 1862, was appointed commander of
the Army of Northern Virginia. Stonewall Jackson once said, "So great
is my confidence in General Lee that I am willing to follow him blind-
folded." Lee is shown here in an 1863 photograph by Julian Vannerson.

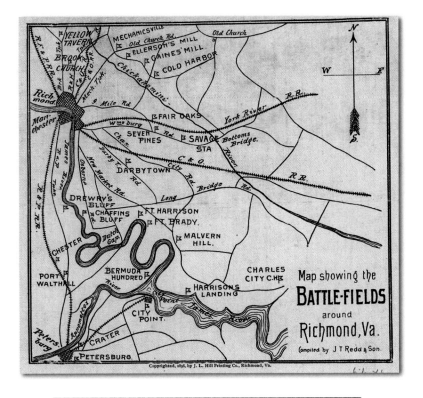

This map, created by J. T. Redd & Son in 1896, shows the Civil War battlefields surrounding Richmond, Virginia. The small crossroads at Mechanicsville, Gaines' Mill, Cold Harbor, Savage's Station, and Malvern Hill, which would see heavy fighting during the Seven Days' Battles, stand in a wide arc around the Confederate capital.

not follow through with his original plan to attack again the next day.

Lee, meanwhile, finalized his plans to attack McClellan's lines north of the Chickahominy River. Jackson's troops would begin their 15-mile (24-km) march early the next morning. The rest of Lee's army would wait for Jackson's attack to signal the start of their movements. Jackson would attack the right of the Federal position, while other Confederate commanders advanced against the right and the center. When day broke on June 26, Jackson's men were not ready on time, and, after many delays, spent the entire day on the march toward the enemy. Other Confederate units waited idly to cooperate with Jackson's attack. Late that afternoon, Confederate general Ambrose Powell Hill impatiently attacked a Federal corps holding a defensive position at Mechanicsville, a crossroads just north of the Chickahominy River. Hill made no progress and lost almost 1,500 men, while the Yankees lost less than 400 men. Jackson's men set up camp for the night without firing a single shot.

Lee, frustrated by the day's events, made plans to attack McClellan again the next day. He ordered Jackson to take command of all the Confederate troops camped north of the Chickahominy River, which amounted to more than half of the Army of Northern Virginia, and to advance 8 miles (12.9 km) southeast to the crossroads at Cold Harbor. There the Confederates would attack the right flank of the Federal lines, between Cold Harbor and the river. Lee's plans required coordination among the eleven Confederate generals. His orders were confusing, his generals' maps were inaccurate, and many of the generals were late in arriving or got lost along the way.

The battle did not begin until the afternoon of June 27, when A. P. Hill's division attacked elements of McClellan's army. The Confederates charged repeatedly, through swampland, against the Federal position but made no progress. Once again, Jackson and his troops were late. When his men finally arrived on the battlefield, they joined in the attack but were unable to break through the Federal lines. One last Rebel charge, led by Jackson's troops, began when it was almost dark. The Yankees, badly outnumbered, were forced back in confusion. This battle, called the Battle of Gaines' Mill for a nearby gristmill, was a Confederate victory, but a very costly one. Lee had lost almost 8,000 Confederates. Some 6,800 Federals were killed or wounded.

In response, McClellan began his retreat, marching southeast toward his base on the James River. Lee followed, close on the Federals' heels. Skirmishes broke out at Savage's Station on June 29 and Glendale on June 30. These battles were indecisive and cost many lives. The Confederates lost some 4,000 men, and the Federals lost about 4,700 men. The Rebels were unable to defeat the Yankees outright, and McClellan continued to retreat, unwilling to risk more lives in full-scale combat.

Jackson's troops did not participate in the Battle of Savage's Station, and they did not play a significant role in the Battle of Glendale. Lee's orders to his generals were increasingly unclear, and his officers did not coordinate their marches and attacks with one another. Jackson, who was both exhausted and sick, lacked the sense of purpose he had displayed in the Shenandoah Valley campaign. His performance was a disappointment.

The Battle of Malvern Hill was the sixth and final battle of the Seven Days' campaign. This sketch of the battle was made by Union private Robert Knox Sneden on July 1, 1862. Although the battle was a Confederate defeat, the Union forces, led by General McClellan, withdrew to the James River, thus ending the Peninsula Campaign. In response, General Lee sent Jackson to fight General Pope's forces near the Rapidan River, initiating the Northern Virginia Campaign.

McClellan withdrew again, heading 2 miles (3 km) south to Malvern Hill, which was 25 miles (40.2 km) southeast of Richmond and not far from the James River. The Federals established a very strong defensive position, strengthened by cannons, atop the hill itself. On July 1, Lee sent the Army of Northern Virginia charging against the Federal lines. As before, his plans were complicated and vague. Confederate cannons were ordered to bombard the Federal cannons on the hill, paving the way for a Rebel infantry charge.

The Confederate bombardment had little effect, but one of Lee's generals thought it had weakened McClellan's infantry enough to order an attack. One Confederate brigade started forward, and the rest of Lee's army followed in small groups, not as the unified force the original plan had called for. The heavy fire from the Federal cannons and rifles was deadly, and the battle ended in bloody failure for the Confederates. By late afternoon, Lee had ordered his men to stop fighting. The Rebels had lost 5,600 men, with almost 900 dead, 4,200 wounded, and more than 500 missing. The Yankees had lost 3,000 men, with 300 dead, almost 1,900 wounded, and 800 missing.

Though the battle of Malvern Hill was a tactical victory for McClellan and the Army of the Potomac, it was also a strategic defeat. McClellan, in spite of his success that day, was determined to continue his retreat all the way to Harrison's Landing, the Federal base 5 miles (8 km) southeast of Malvern Hill on the James River. The campaign was finished. In seven days of hard fighting, the Army of Northern Virginia had pushed the Yankee invaders away from Richmond and had saved the Confederate capital, at least for the moment. The campaign was the bloodiest of the war so far. More than twenty thousand Confederates and more than fifteen thousand Federals had been killed, wounded, or captured. Unionists and Confederates were shocked by the death toll.

Jackson's performance that week was the most disappointing of his career. However, many southern soldiers and civilians, ignorant of what had actually occurred and influenced by Jackson's popularity after the Shenandoah Valley campaign, assumed that Jackson had been largely responsible for the Confederate victory. In July 1862, an admiring Rebel soldier wrote, "some of our boys says that they wish all the yankees ware in hell but I dont for if they ware to go there Old Jackson would follow them there to[o]."

McClellan was soon ordered to return to Washington, D.C. Officials there decided to organize a new Federal army, the Army of Virginia, to capture Richmond. The Union force was commanded by General John Pope, and its numbers grew steadily. Lee responded by sending Jackson and the Left Wing of the Army of Northern Virginia toward Pope's army.

On August 9, 1862, Jackson's Confederates encountered part of Pope's army near Cedar Mountain, Virginia, a small ridge about 60 miles (96.6 km) north of Richmond and about 70 miles (112.7 km) east of Washington, D.C. Nathaniel P. Banks, Jackson's old foe from the Shenandoah Valley campaign, commanded the Federal division there. Jackson's total force outnumbered Banks's troops by about two to one, but some of the Confederates were still on the way when the battle began.

The Confederates charged the Federals a few units at a time but made no real progress. Banks sent a fierce counterattack against Jackson's left flank. Before long some Confederate units were barely holding on, others were falling back slowly, and others were starting to run from the battlefield. To inspire his weary soldiers, Jackson rode to the front of the Confederate lines, waving his sword in one hand and a battle flag in the other and shouting, "Jackson is with you. . . . Rally, men! . . . Forward, men, forward!" The Confederates nearby gathered in tight formation, and, as the rest of Jackson's force arrived on the battlefield, his men made an inspired counterattack. By the end of the day, the Rebels had forced the Yankees to retreat. The Rebels were victorious at the Battle of Cedar Mountain, but the fight was not important in a strategic sense.

Jackson's recent failures and narrow victories had almost no effect on his reputation as a great general, however. Newspapers provided inaccurate accounts of what he had done. Most southern civilians and Jackson's own troops had complete faith in him. A captain who had served under Jackson since the Shenandoah Valley campaign wrote to his wife soon after the Battle of Cedar Mountain, claiming proudly that Jackson was "one of the greatest men living."

Just two weeks later, Jackson would prove that the Confederacy's faith in him was not unfounded. Lee

Next spread: Edwin Forbes sketched the battle of Cedar Mountain. The Confederates nearly suffered defeat in the battle, but won in the end. This resulted in the fighting in Virginia shifting from the peninsula to Northern Virginia. The battle was the last time Jackson led the Army of Northern Virginia.

feared that McClellan's army would be ordered to reinforce Pope's force, making a combined Federal force more than 100,000 men strong. Lee decided to move against Pope's army once again before McClellan could join it. Pope held a position just north of the Rappahannock River, about halfway between Richmond and Washington, D.C. Lee planned to send Jackson on a long march north of Pope's right flank and behind the Federals, intercepting the Federal supply line at the railroad station at Manassas Junction. Meanwhile the rest of the Confederate army, under

General James Longstreet, would distract Pope by engaging his forces on the Rappahannock River. If all went well, the Confederates would force a Federal retreat to Washington, D.C.

Jackson and his force left their camp northeast of Cedar Mountain early on the morning of August 25, 1862. In just two days, they marched 56 miles (90.1 km) in a long arc, heading first northwest, then northeast, and finally southeast toward Manassas Junction. On August 27, they arrived there, about 10 miles (16.1 km) northeast of Pope's army. The Confederates captured several railroad cars full of supplies, including food, clothing, and equipment. Jackson ordered his troops to burn what they could not carry with them and to withdraw to a position at Groveton. Groveton was a small crossroads near the battlefield of Bull Run, which had seen fierce fighting the previous July. Pope arrived at Manassas Junction that afternoon and found the smoking remains of the supplies the enemy had destroyed. Pope ordered his units to concentrate at Centreville, 7 miles (11.3 km) north of the junction. Jackson, meanwhile, knew that Lee and Longstreet were somewhere near Thoroughfare Gap, about 10 miles (16.1 km) west and about a ten-hour march away. He waited for an opportunity to draw Pope into battle, believing he could hold the Federals' attention long enough for Lee and Longstreet to arrive.

Early in the evening of August 28, Jackson got his chance. He observed one of Pope's divisions marching by on Warrenton Turnpike, the road running northeast past Jackson's camp. The Confederates unleashed a stunning attack on the unsuspecting Federals. Rebels and Yankees stood in lines as close as 50 yards (45.7 m) apart and fired repeatedly for two and one-half hours. A Confederate officer later called the battle "a blaze of fire," and a Federal officer described the sound of rifles firing as "a long and continuous roll." Groveton was not a large-scale battle, nor was it a long one, but the combat there was ferocious. The fighting ended at nightfall.

The Confederates had lost 1,200 men, and the Federals had lost 1,100 men.

General Pope and the rest of the Army of Virginia arrived on August 29. Pope ordered his men to press forward, and the fighting continued most of the day. Every time the Federals charged the Confederate lines, it seemed as if Jackson's men were about to be defeated, but somehow the Confederates managed to force the Federals back. When some Confederates ran out of bullets, they picked up rocks and

Union General John Pope was photographed at the Mathew Brady Studio between 1860 and 1865. Pope was relieved of his command after losing the Second Battle of Bull Run, and was sent to Minnesota to put down a Sioux Indian uprising.

threw them at their enemies. Fresh Confederate troops, under Longstreet, arrived just in time to force the Federals to retreat back to their original lines. By the time fighting ended at dark, Lee and the rest of the Army of Northern Virginia had arrived on the battlefield.

Pope believed that the Confederates would withdraw to Richmond. He was wrong. On the afternoon of August 30, the Federals attacked Jackson again, and the Confederates held on and forced Pope's men back once again. Lee sent Jackson and Longstreet forward together in a counterattack that caught Pope by surprise.

Though the Yankees tried to resist, they were over-whelmed. Their retreat went smoothly at first, but soon many of Pope's men ran away in a panic. The battle ended on the hill where Jackson and his brigade had earned the nickname Stonewall in the First Battle of Bull Run the year before. The Yankees withdrew toward Washington, D.C., and the Rebels pursued them until nightfall.

This battle, called the Second Battle of Bull Run by the Federals and the Second Battle of Manassas by the Confederates, was another embarrassing defeat for the Union. Southern morale was high. Confederate generals and civilian officials believed the time was right for Rebel armies to invade Yankee territory. A victory over a Union army on northern soil might con-vince England and France to recognize the

On the afternoon of August 30, 1862, Edwin Forbes sketched this Bull Run battle scene from the slope of a nearby hill. In the middle ground, John Pope's front line meets Thomas Jackson's wing of the Confederate army.

Confederacy as an independent country and to offer economic and military aid to fight the war.

Abraham Lincoln, frustrated at Pope's failure, relieved the general of his command, transferred units from the Army of Virginia back to McClellan's Army of the Potomac, and gave McClellan another chance against Lee. McClellan was a cautious general, one who always believed that he was greatly outnumbered by the enemy and who hesitated to order his troops to march or fight. With slightly fewer troops than he had during the Seven Days' Battles, McClellan returned to command facing a very confident Lee.

On September 4, 1862, Lee crossed the Potomac River into Maryland, splitting his army in two. He ordered Jackson on a long march to capture the Federal force guarding the town of Harpers Ferry. The rest of the Army of Northern Virginia, under Generals Longstreet and Daniel Harvey Hill, marched northwest, still farther into Maryland. McClellan, meanwhile, slowly marched from Washington, D.C., reaching the town of Frederick, Maryland, two days after the Confederates had left it.

There a Yankee soldier found a copy of Lee's orders outlining his plans for the campaign, and he took them to his colonel, who delivered them to McClellan. The Federal commander had been given one of the greatest opportunities in military history, but he characteristically wasted valuable time before marching in pursuit of the enemy. After a Rebel spy informed Lee that

McClellan had a copy of the Confederate orders, Lee quickly made plans to reunite the scattered elements of his army. On September 15, Jackson captured the town of Harpers Ferry. He left two divisions behind to watch the Yankee prisoners and to take charge of the captured supplies, then he raced north to join Lee.

Lee did not want to retreat to Virginia without fighting a full-scale battle, even though he knew that in doing so he took a great risk. He decided to concentrate the Army of Northern Virginia at the town of Sharpsburg, Maryland, 18 miles (29 km) west of Frederick and 9 miles (14.5 km) north of Harpers Ferry. The Confederates, with only 26,000 men, set up a defensive line just west of the town along Antietam Creek. Lee was almost daring McClellan to attack him, even though the Union's 75,000-man force outnumbered the Confederates almost three to one.

Early on the morning of September 17, McClellan attacked Lee. So began the bloodiest day of the Civil War. Jackson's wing, short two divisions that were still on the way from Harpers Ferry, was on the Confederate left. The Yankees attacked him first, launching a series of head-on charges against the Rebel lines. Jackson, with only three divisions facing an entire corps, held his ground and even waged several counterattacks, but he could not drive the Federals away.

After about four hours of fighting, and just as Jackson's line was about to break, McClellan shifted his attention to the center of Lee's line, where Daniel Harvey Hill defended a sunken road that would come to be called Bloody Lane. Federal charges hammered against the Confederate line until it seemed as if it would surely collapse. After another four hours of bloody combat, McClellan shifted his attention to the Confederate right, held by Longstreet. Late that afternoon, as the Federals pushed Longstreet's line to the breaking point, Jackson's last division, commanded by Ambrose Powell Hill, arrived on the battlefield. It forced the Federals back just in time to save Lee's army from almost certain defeat. McClellan, who for some reason had not ordered all his available troops into battle, withdrew his men a short distance east and left the Rebels on the battlefield.

Both armies, exhausted by twelve hours of fighting and shocked by the incredible numbers of dead and wounded, spent the next day waiting for the enemy to renew the fight. When neither commander did, the campaign was finished. The Confederates retreated to Virginia two days later. The battle, which the Federals named the Battle of Antietam for the nearby creek, and which the Confederates named the Battle of Sharpsburg

Next spread: Alexander Gardner photographed Antietam Creek in the days after the battle. The battered fences and dusty roads are signs of the recent conflict. In an 1866 book of photographs, Gardner wrote of the field at Antietam, "Houses and fences have been repaired, harvests have ripened over the breasts of the fallen, and the ploughshare only now and then turns up a shot, as a relic of that great struggle."

for the town close by, was the bloodiest day in all of American history. More than 23,000 men on both sides were killed, wounded, missing, or captured. The Union and Confederate armies in Virginia spent the next months maneuvering or resting from the hard campaigns of the spring and summer.

Lee reorganized the Army of Northern Virginia into two large corps and promoted both Longstreet and Jackson to lieutenant general in October. Longstreet commanded the First Corps, and Jackson commanded the Second Corps. In early November 1862, the Second Corps moved to a camp near Millwood, a village 11 miles (17.7 km) east of Winchester. By that time it had been almost nine months since Jackson had seen his wife, Anna. Just before Jackson had embarked on the Shenandoah Valley campaign, the couple had learned that Anna was going to have a baby. On November 23, she gave birth to a girl. Jackson, who learned of the baby's birth by letter, was relieved to read that both mother and child were in excellent health. The Jacksons named their daughter Julia for her paternal grandmother.

The Federals in the Army of the Potomac, meanwhile, had stayed in Maryland for more than a month after the Battle of Antietam. General McClellan, unwilling to pursue Lee, did not cross the Potomac River into Virginia until the end of October. He mistakenly believed that Lee's Confederate troops outnumbered his own army, and he made repeated excuses for not moving or fighting.

President Abraham Lincoln, increasingly frustrated by McClellan's ineffective leadership, replaced him with General Ambrose E. Burnside in the first week of November. Burnside was anxious to prove he was the right man to command the Army of the Potomac. His army, numbering 120,000 Federals, was camped near Warrenton, Virginia, about 45 miles (72.4 km) southwest of Washington, D.C. Burnside ordered his Yankees to

Thomas Jackson adored children. Having suffered the deaths of two children, Jackson was relieved to learn of the healthy birth of his daughter Julia, shown here with her mother in a photograph taken after Jackson's death.

Fredericksburg, Virginia, a city about halfway between Washington, D.C., and Richmond. From there he planned to advance on the Confederate capital of Richmond itself.

The Army of the Potomac reached Fredericksburg by the middle of November. The Army of Northern Virginia, its largest yet with some 78,500 Confederate troops, awaited the Yankees there. Lee's lines, west of the town, stretched southeast from the Rappahannock

River to Hamilton's Crossing. The left and center of the Rebel line was atop Marye's Heights, a ridge overlooking Fredericksburg.

On the morning of December 13, 1862, Burnside launched a two-pronged attack through thick fog. His first attempt was against the Confederate right, where Jackson's Second Corps was posted in woods near the railroad line at Hamilton's Crossing. After a brief exchange between artillery, one Federal corps advanced against Jackson's lines and briefly broke through them. A Confederate counterattack pushed the Federals back beyond the railroad, but a Federal counterattack in response pushed the Confederates back to their original position. Fighting on that part of the field continued until midafternoon.

Burnside then ordered two Federal corps to charge across an open field that rose for 400 yards (365.8 m) up the hills west of Fredericksburg. The Confederates in Longstreet's First Corps were posted on the high ground just below Marye's Heights. They were supported by a long line of artillerists. Fifteen brigades of Burnside's Yankees charged the field six separate times between noon and nightfall. The Confederates rebuffed each attack. Thousands of Federal soldiers fell, dead or wounded, and few came within 150 yards (137.2 m) of the well-protected Confederate lines.

Burnside wanted to attack again the next morning, but his generals convinced him that further fighting

This Arthur Lumley drawing, created in 1862, shows Union soldiers carrying a wounded soldier on a stretcher during the Battle of Fredericksburg.

would be pointless. The Battle of Fredericksburg was a decisive Confederate victory and one of the most one-sided battles of the war. Burnside had lost 12,600 men in the battle, with 1,300 dead, 9,600 wounded, and 1,700 missing. Two-thirds of them, or 8,800, were lost in the futile charges against Marye's Heights. Lee had lost only 4,200 men. The two armies soon settled into winter camp and would not fight again until spring. In May 1863, Robert E. Lee would win his greatest battle, and Stonewall Jackson would be the reason why.

9. Marching to Glory

Thomas Jackson and the Second Corps set up winter camp at a nearby plantation named Moss Neck. There Jackson worked with his staff officers to write official reports. He also read and wrote letters, and ordered rations and supplies. Every Sunday Jackson went to services at a log chapel nearby, and many of his men not only admired his devotion to God but also shared his faith. Jackson was so popular that people around the world wrote to him asking for his autograph or a lock of his hair. They sent him presents, such as boxes of food and bottles of wine, handkerchiefs and gloves, saddles and blankets, and even a horse. Jackson wrote to Anna that these gifts were proof of God's blessings.

At the end of January 1863, Abraham Lincoln replaced Ambrose E. Burnside, whose Fredericksburg campaign had been a disaster, with General Joseph Hooker. Hooker took an army worn out and discouraged by the campaigns of 1862 and soon transformed it into an efficient fighting force. Lee's Army of Northern Virginia, meanwhile, was about half the size of the Army of the Potomac. Almost all of James Longstreet's First Corps were on detached duty in southern Virginia and would not rejoin the army for several weeks. Yet Lee's Rebels were even more confident than the Yankees were, believing wholeheartedly in their famous commander.

In March 1863, the Second Corps left Moss Neck and encamped a few miles (km) northwest. As the start of the spring campaign approached, Jackson enjoyed a few of the happiest days of his life with Anna and their daughter, Julia, who visited the

A confident General Joseph Hooker proudly called the Army of the Potomac "the finest army the sun ever shone on . . . May God have mercy on General Lee, for I will have none."

troops in winter quarters. Jackson and Anna were thrilled to be together again, and he was especially pleased to hold Julia in his arms. The five-month-old baby was baptized by Reverend B. T. Lacy, chaplain of the Second Corps, during the short visit.

Only a few days after his wife and baby's arrival, however, Jackson's attention returned to the war. The Federals had made the first move of the spring campaign. The Army of the Potomac was crossing the Rappahannock River at Fredericksburg and advancing south. Hooker thought that other Union generals had been too cautious. He had decided to attack the Army of Northern Virginia, hoping to catch the Confederates by surprise. Kissing Anna and Julia good-bye and sending them back to the safety of Richmond, Jackson went to meet with Lee. The Confederates soon rushed units toward a little crossroads called Chancellorsville, 9 miles (14.5 km) west.

Chancellorsville was not a town at all, but a small open space in a forest so thick with trees, bushes, and vines that it was called the Wilderness. Lee and Jackson knew that Hooker's force outnumbered their own, but they also knew that if they attacked him first, they would have the advantage. Engaging Hooker in the thick forest would also improve their chances. It would be difficult for Hooker to shift his units from point to point in response to Lee's movements.

On May 1, 1863, the Rebels attacked the advancing Yankees. In response, Hooker led his troops deeper into the Wilderness, laid out a defensive line, and waited. Lee and Jackson soon discovered that Hooker's line was unprotected on one flank. Lee ordered Jackson to take most of the Army of Northern Virginia on a long march around and behind Hooker's line. Jackson would attack the Yankees from the right and rear while Lee attacked them from the front. Jackson spent most of the night planning the 12-mile (19.3-km) route that wound its way southwest, then northwest, then back east through the Wilderness to a point beyond the end of Hooker's line.

Shortly before sunrise on May 2, Jackson and Lee met to discuss Jackson's bold plan. They sat on wooden

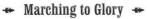

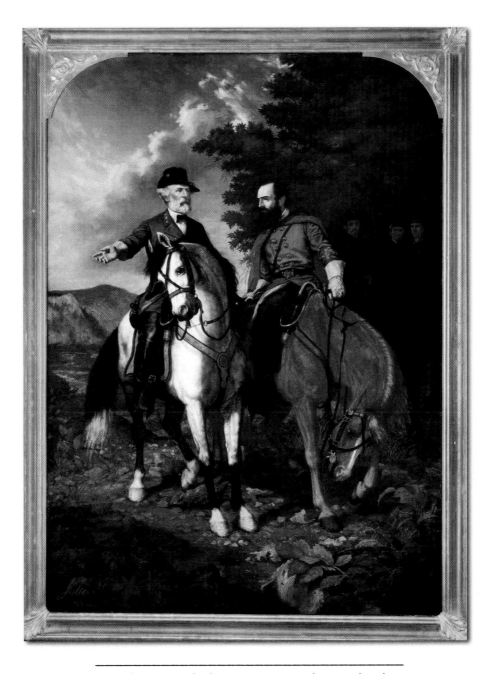

Everett B. D. Julio painted *The Last Meeting of Lee and Jackson* in 1869. The painting dramatically depicts the two generals conferring near the Wilderness outside Chancellorsville. The generals decided to make a daring move and split their troops several times. They took Hooker's Union troops by surprise.

cracker boxes in a clearing. Lee would be left with only one-third of his army, or less than 15,000 Confederates, to face the entire Army of the Potomac, which numbered 120,000 Federals. Jackson would take two-thirds of the Army of Northern Virginia on a difficult march that might decide the battle. Lee considered the plan for a few moments. Then, expressing his confidence in Jackson, he said, "Well, go on."

The Second Corps started on the march early that morning. Jackson's men had orders to march as quickly as possible. By midafternoon, the Rebels reached the end of the Union line and began to make the formation for their surprise attack. Hooker's men were relaxing at camp, cooking dinner, and writing letters home. Suddenly the Confederates crashed through the woods, screaming the rebel yell. Their attack drove most of a Federal corps back in confusion, causing a stampede among the Yankees. Some Federal soldiers, trying desperately to reach safety, ran as far away as 2 miles (3.2 km). Others stayed to fight, but they faced a tidal wave of Confederate attackers. "Never did troops fight better than ours or worse than the Yankees," one Confederate soldier wrote to his father a few days later. The fighting ended only with nightfall. Jackson quietly urged, "Press on! Press on!" but his soldiers could do no more that day.

Later that night, Jackson rode ahead of the Confederate lines, along narrow roads in the Wilderness, searching for a route behind Hooker's

Civil War sketch artist Alfred R. Waud shows the Eleventh Corps of the Union army in a chaotic retreat at the Battle of Chancellorsville. When a fellow Confederate officer told Jackson of the Yankee retreat, saying, "General, they are running too fast for us; we can't come up with them," Jackson answered, "They never run too fast for me, sir."

army. Jackson hoped to maneuver his troops into position overnight and block any Federal retreat staged the following day. As Jackson and his staff officers returned to camp later that night, Rebels of the Second Corps heard hoofbeats and mistakenly thought the group was Yankee cavalry. They fired blindly in the direction of the noise. "You are firing into your own men!" one of Jackson's staff officers yelled. "It's a lie!" a Confederate infantry officer yelled back. "Pour it to them, boys!"

Jackson was wounded twice in the left arm and once in the right hand. It took several hours to carry Jackson out of the Wilderness and to a field hospital. There Dr. Hunter H. McGuire, chief surgeon of the Second Corps, examined Jackson closely. The wounds in Jackson's left arm were serious. To prevent infection and possibly save Jackson's life, his wounded arm would have to be amputated, or cut off. The operation took almost an hour. McGuire then sent Jackson to Fairfield, a plantation 12 miles (19.3 km) southeast of Fredericksburg, where the general could get good medical care and rest.

The heaviest fighting of the battle occurred the next morning, May 3, near the Chancellorsville crossroads. Confederates, who had heard that Jackson had been wounded, charged the Federals shouting "Remember Jackson!" Several determined Confederate attacks, closely supported by artillery, drove the Federals back from the crossroads. Hooker had had enough. Over the next few days, he withdrew the Army of the Potomac. Years later Hooker would say, "for once I lost confidence in Hooker, and that is all there is to it."

The Battle of Chancellorsville was Robert E. Lee's greatest victory, but it was won at a terrible cost. It was Stonewall Jackson's last fight. Dr. McGuire did all he could, but Jackson got weaker every day. He took powerful medicine to help ease his pain, and, as a result, he slept most of the time. When he was awake, he talked about the war, God, and his chances for getting well.

Sometimes, however, Jackson drifted into a confused state and began to give orders as if he were still on the battlefield. When Anna got the news that her husband had been injured, she left Richmond, arriving at Fairfield on May 7. She was shocked to see Jackson so ill. He tried to comfort her and to convince her that whatever happened would be according to God's will. "I am not afraid to die," he said more than once, and then tried to encourage Anna by adding, "I may yet get well." People across the Confederacy prayed for Jackson's recovery.

By Sunday, May 10, 1863, Stonewall Jackson's condition had worsened, probably from a combination of pneumonia and an infection in one of his

In nineteenth-century America, doctors did not understand the causes of infection or disease, and they had few medicines to give to the sick. If a soldier was shot in the head, chest, or stomach, he usually died. If he was shot in the arm or the leg, surgeons would often cut off the limb with a saw. Bullets shattered bones and wounds got infected easily. If an infection spread from a wound to the rest of the body, the soldier usually died. Some 360,000 Yankees and 250,000 Rebels either were killed or died of disease during the Civil War. About twice as many soldiers died of disease as died in battle. They died from diseases and conditions such as measles, smallpox, typhoid fever, malaria, diarrhea, and dysentery.

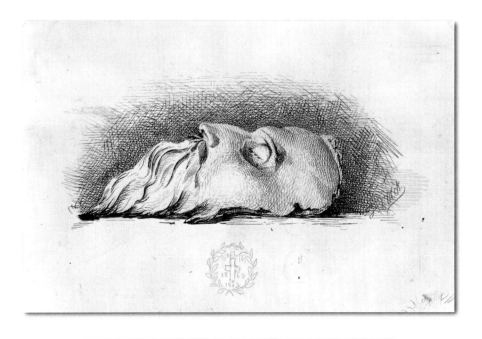

Adalbert J. Volck made a sketch of Jackson's death mask around 1863. A death mask is a casting, usually plaster, of a person's face, made after the person has died. These masks were often made for and kept by family members to remember their loved ones.

wounds. Jackson asked McGuire if he was going to die that day, saying that he would not mind dying on a Sunday. McGuire told Jackson that he probably would die before the end of the day. "Very good, very good," Jackson answered. "It is all right." Later that afternoon, Jackson began to drift in and out of consciousness. He revived briefly, excitedly imagining himself back at the Battle of Chancellorsville and giving orders to his staff officers. He then became calm, sensing that the end was near. He said, "Let us cross over the river and rest under the shade of the trees," then he died.

10. Stonewall Jackson and His Legacy

The day after Thomas Jackson died, Robert E. Lee wrote to his son Custis, "It is a terrible loss. I do not know how to replace him." How would the Confederacy push on without the mighty Stonewall?

In the summer of 1863, Lee led the Army of Northern Virginia across the Potomac River for a second invasion of the North. His troops lost a bloody battle at Gettysburg, Pennsylvania. As the war dragged on for the rest of 1863, through 1864, and into early 1865, the Army of Northern Virginia took a more defensive role and lost more battles and more men. Lee was finally forced to give up the cause in order to save the lives of thousands of Confederate soldiers. He surrendered to the Army of the Potomac, led by U. S. Grant, at Appomattox Courthouse, Virginia, on April 9, 1865. Other Confederate armies surrendered soon after, and the war came to an end.

During the final years of the war, Jackson's reputation only grew. His victories in the Shenandoah Valley campaign, which had come when Confederate morale was terribly low, inspired Southerners to believe that

Rebel forces could defeat Yankee armies. He had won victories when his army had fewer soldiers and more miles to march than his enemies did. He was admired for his determination, his perseverance, and his devotion to God and the Southern cause. In the beginning, the Jackson myth was based largely on fact, focusing on his brilliant generalship in the Shenandoah Valley. Soon, however, public perceptions of him became so exaggerated that it is sometimes still hard to separate fact from fiction. Today, Stonewall Jackson is remembered as one of the

A group of young women gather to mourn at Jackson's grave in a photograph from around 1866. There was a great outpouring of emotion across the Confederacy at the news of Jackson's death. One Confederate officer wrote in a letter to his sister, "We never knew how much we all loved him until he died." A soldier in the ranks wrote, "We lost the best general we had in the field that mighty Stonewall Jackson."

The likenesses of (*left to right*) Jefferson Davis, Robert E. Lee, and Thomas Jonathan Jackson are carved into the side of Stone Mountain, a Confederate memorial in Georgia.

greatest generals in American history. We continue to tell stories of his unlikely successes and his tragic death, stories that will be told as long as historians write about the Civil War.

Timeline

1824   Thomas Jackson is born in Clarksburg, Virginia (modern-day West Virginia).

1846   Jackson graduates from the U.S. Military Academy at West Point.

1846–1851   Jackson serves as an officer in the U.S. Army in the Mexican War and at posts in New York and Florida.

1851   Jackson becomes a professor at the Virginia Military Institute in Lexington.

1853   Jackson marries Elinor Junkin.

1854   Elinor Jackson dies after giving birth to a stillborn baby.

1857   Jackson marries Mary Anna Morrison.

1861   On April 26, two weeks after the Civil War begins, Jackson is made a colonel in the Virginia state forces.

On June 17, Jackson is made a brigadier general in the Confederate army.

On July 21, at the Battle of Bull Run (Manassas), Jackson earns the nickname Stonewall.

On October 7, Jackson is promoted to major general. He is soon given command of the Army of the Valley, defending the Shenandoah Valley of Virginia.

1861–1862   From December 1861 to January 1862, Jackson commands an unsuccessful expedition in the mountains of western Virginia.

1862   From March to June, Jackson's Army of the Valley faces several Union armies in the Shenandoah Valley.

On March 23, Jackson is defeated by General James Shields in the Battle of Kernstown.

On May 8, Jackson defeats General Robert Milroy in the Battle of McDowell. On May 23, Jackson defeats a smaller Union force at Front Royal. On May 25, he defeats General Nathaniel P. Banks in the Battle of Winchester.

Jackson divides his army and defeats Union generals John C. Frémont at Cross Keys on June 8, and James Shields at Port Republic on June 9, thus ending the Shenandoah Valley campaign. In late June, Jackson is ordered to join General Robert E. Lee's Army of Northern Virginia near Richmond. From June 25 to July 1, Jackson takes part in the Seven Days' Battles against General George B. McClellan's Army of the Potomac.

On August 9, Jackson defeats Nathaniel P. Banks in the Battle of Cedar Mountain. On August 29–30, Jackson takes part in the Confederate victory over General John Pope's Army of Virginia at the Second Battle of Bull Run (Manassas).

Jackson forces the capture of the Union forces at Harpers Ferry on September 15. On September 17, Jackson plays a major role in the Battle of Antietam (Sharpsburg) against McClellan and the Army of the Potomac.

On October 11, Jackson is promoted to lieutenant general and given command of the Second Corps of the Army of Northern Virginia.

On November 23, Thomas and Mary Anna Jackson's daughter, Julia, is born.

On December 13, Jackson's corps plays a minor role in defeating General Ambrose E. Burnside and the Army of the Potomac at the Battle of Fredericksburg.

1863   On May 2, Jackson leads the successful Confederate attack on General Joseph Hooker's Army of the Potomac at the Battle of Chancellorsville. That night, Jackson is accidentally wounded by his own soldiers.

On May 10, Jackson dies at Fairfield, a plantation near Guinea Station, Virginia.

Glossary

arsenal (AR-sih-nul) A storehouse of weapons.

battery (BA-tuh-ree) A group of cannons.

casualties (KA-zhul-teez) The number of soldiers killed, wounded, or captured in battle.

Confederate (kun-FEH-duh-ret) Relating to people who fought for the South in the Civil War.

conscientious (kon-she-EN-shus) Careful, moral.

constable (KON-stuh-bul) A minor court officer, sometimes the equal of a policeman.

controversial (kon-truh-VUR-shul) Causing disagreement.

denomination (dih-nah-meh-NAY-shun) A group of churches that share the same beliefs and join together.

detached (dih-TACHT) Separate, away from the assigned group.

eccentric (ik-SEN-trik) Strange, different from established custom or style.

exaggerated (eg-ZAH-juh-rayt-ed) Stretched beyond the truth.

expertise (ek-sper-TEES) The skill of an expert.

ferocious (feh-ROH-shus) Fierce, extremely intense.

garrison (GAR-ih-sun) The troops stationed at a fort or other military post.

gristmill (GRIST-mil) A mill for grinding grain.

honeymoon (HUH-nee-moon) A trip or vacation taken by a newly married couple.

maneuvering (muh-NOO-ver-ing) Moving into or out of position for a purpose.

mineralogy (mih-neh-RAH-luh-jee) The science dealing with minerals, their properties, their classification, and distinguishing between them.

morale (muh-RAL) The mental and emotional feeling of a person or a group about the task at hand.

natural philosophy (NA-chuh-rul fih-LAH-suh-fee) Any of the sciences that deal with matter or energy, such as physics, chemistry, or biology.

persevered (per-seh-VEERD) Continued with an action or undertaking despite opposition or discouragement.

plebe (PLEEB) A first-year student in a military or naval academy.

ploughshare (PLOW-sher) A part of the plow that cuts the furrow, or trench, in which seeds will be planted. The modern spelling is plowshare.

prosecution (prah-sih-KYOO-shun) Legal action taken against someone for the purpose of punishment.

reinforced (ree-in-FORSD) Attacked or defended with additional soldiers.

secede (sih-SEED) To withdraw from a group or a country.

shoals (SHOHLZ) Large groups or numbers, crowds.

stampede (stam-PEED) A wild rush of frightened people.

strategic (struh-TEE-jik) Related to the science of planning and directing large military movements.

tactics (TAK-tiks) The movement of forces into the best position before and during a battle.

treason (TREE-zun) The crime of attempting to overthrow one's own government.

tuberculosis (too-ber-kyuh-LOH-sis) A serious infectious disease that affects the lungs.

typhoid fever (TY-foyd FEE-ver) An infectious and often deadly disease that is usually caused by unclean food and water.

Additional Resources

To learn more about Stonewall Jackson, check out the following books and Web sites:

Books

Monsell, Helen A. *Tom Jackson: Young Stonewall*. Childhood of Famous Americans Series. Indianapolis: Bobbs-Merrill, 1942.

Robertson, James I., Jr. *Standing Like a Stone Wall: The Life of General Thomas J. Jackson*. New York: Simon & Schuster, 2001.

Wheeler, Richard. *We Knew Stonewall Jackson*. New York: Crowell, 1977.

Web Sites

Due to the changing nature of Internet links, PowerPlus Books has developed an online list of Web sites related to the subject of this book. This site is updated regularly. Please use this link to access the list:
www.powerkidslinks.com/lalt/stonewall/

Bibliography

Arnold, Thomas Jackson. *Early Life and Letters of General Thomas J. Jackson ("Stonewall" Jackson)*. New York: Fleming H. Revell Company, 1916.

Chambers, Lenoir. *Stonewall Jackson*. 2 vols. New York: William Morrow, 1959.

Cooke, John Esten. *Stonewall Jackson and the Old Stonewall Brigade*. Edited by Richard Barksdale Harwell. Charlottesville, VA: University of Virginia Press, 1954.

Freeman, Douglas Southall. *Lee's Lieutenants: A Study In Command*. 3 vols. New York: Charles Scribner's Sons, 1942–1944.

Jackson, Mary Anna. *Memoirs of Stonewall Jackson by his Widow Mary Anna Jackson*. Louisville, KY: Courier-Journal Job Printing Company, 1895.

Robertson, James I., Jr. *The Stonewall Brigade*. Baton Rouge, LA: Louisiana State University Press, 1962.

Robertson, James I., Jr. *Stonewall Jackson: The Man, the Soldier, the Legend*. New York: Macmillan, 1997.

Vandiver, Frank E. *Mighty Stonewall*. New York: McGraw-Hill, 1957.

Index

About the Author

J. Tracy Power is a historian with the South Carolina Department of Archives and History in Columbia, South Carolina. A native Georgian who has lived in South Carolina since 1981, Power received his B.A. in history from Emory University and his M.A. and Ph.D. in history from the University of South Carolina. He works to document and interpret historic sites in South Carolina through the National Register of Historic Places and the South Carolina Historical Marker Program. He has also taught history at Midlands Technical College and the University of South Carolina. Power is the author of many publications on the Civil War, including the award-winning book *Lee's Miserables: Life in the Army of Northern Virginia from the Wilderness to Appomattox*, and the co-editor of *The Leverett Letters: Correspondence of a South Carolina Family, 1851–1868*.

Primary Sources

Cover (portrait). *General "Stonewall" Jackson, C.S.A.*, circa 1863, Mathew Brady Studio, Virginia Military Institute Archives. **Cover (background).** *Colonel Burnside's Brigade at Bull Run*, drawing on green paper, pencil, Chinese white, and black ink wash, created July 21, 1861, published in the August 5, 1861 *New York Illustrated News*, Alfred R. Waud (1828–1891), Prints and Photographs Division, Library of Congress. **Page 4.** *Thomas Jonathan Jackson*, oil-on-canvas painting, circa 1863, John Adams Elder, © The Corcoran Gallery of Art/CORBIS. **Page 8.** *Jonathan Jackson*, watercolor on ivory, circa 1817, courtesy of the Stonewall Jackson House. The portrait was created as a wedding portrait for Jonathan's bride, Julia Beckwith Neale. **Page 10.** *Laura Jackson Arnold* (1826–1911), carte de visite, Partridge's Gallery, Wheeling, West Virginia. Courtesy of the Stonewall Jackson House. A carte de visite is a type of calling card that was popular in the mid-nineteenth century. **Page 14.** *View of West Point*, oil-on-canvas painting, circa 1835, Thomas Chambers, West Point Museum Art Collection, United States Military Academy. **Page 15.** *Le Cadet*, pen-and-ink drawing, 1842, Cadet George Horatio Derby (1823–1861), Class of 1846, West Point Museum Art Collection, United States Military Academy. Derby was later known as John Phoenix, and was a humorist. **Page 19.** *General Winfield Scott*, gold-toned daguerreotype, circa 1849, Mathew Brady (1823?–1896). Library of Congress Prints and Photographs Division. A daguerreotype is an early type of photograph. The process was invented in the 1830s, and became popular in the mid-nineteenth century. **Page 23.** *Lieutenant Thomas Jackson, U.S. Army*, ambrotype, August 20, 1847, courtesy of the Stonewall Jackson House. Ambrotypes are similar to daguerreotypes, but are made on glass instead of metal. **Page 26.** *Letter from Thomas Jackson to his sister Laura Arnold*, April 1, 1850, New York, Virginia Military Institute Archives. **Page 29.** *Virginia Military Institute*, hand-colored engraving, 1857, Casimir Bohn, Virginia Military Institute Archives. This engraving shows how VMI looked in 1857. **Page 31.** *North Main Street, Lexington, Virginia*, stereocard, circa 1867–1870, Boude & Miley, Rockbridge Historical Society, Photograph Collection. Special Collections, Leyburn Library, Washington and Lee University, Lexington, Virginia. **Page 33.** *Elinor Junkin* (1825–1854), Thomas Jackson's first wife, carte de visite, courtesy of the Stonewall Jackson House Museum. **Page 35.** *Thomas Jackson*, daguerreotype, 1855, H. B. Hull, National Portrait Gallery, Smithsonian Institution/Art Resource, New York. **Page 36.** *Mary Anna Morrison* (1831–1915), Thomas Jackson's second wife, photograph, Virginia Military Institute Archives. **Page 40.** *John Brown Brought Out for Execution*, pencil on paper, 1859, Albert Berghaus, National Portrait Gallery, S.I./Art Resource New York. Berghaus was a sketch artist for *Frank Leslie's Illustrated Newspaper* and made this drawing on December 2, 1859. Brown was being taken to his execution. This sketch appeared as a wood-block engraving in Leslie's newspaper on December 17, 1859. **Page 41.** *Abraham Lincoln* (1809–1865), photograph, 1860, Alexander Hesler, Prints and Photographs Division, Library of Congress. **Page 42.** *Fort Sumter, South Carolina, under the Confederate flag*, photograph, April 14, 1861, Still Picture Branch, National Archives and Records Administration. **Page 45.** *Enfield rifle*, Division of the History of Technology, Armed Forces History, National Museum of American History, S.I. Both armies imported

European firearms to arm their troops. The most widely used was the British Pattern 1853 Enfield rifle-musket, because it was accurate and well made. **Page 46 (right).** *Private Thomas Taylor, Company K, 8th Louisiana Infantry, C.S.A.*, copyprint of an original ambrotype, The Museum of the Confederacy, Richmond, Virginia. **Page 48.** *The Soldierly Bee (*Brigadier General Bernard Bee, C.S.A.), oil sketch, Conrad Wise Chapman, Hampton, Virginia, Valentine Richmond History Center. **Page 50.** *Bull Run, Virginia, Federal cavalry at Sudley Ford,* photograph, created July 1861, published March 1862, George N. Barnard, Prints and Photographs Division, Library of Congress. In the foreground, Confederate children on the riverbank watch the soldiers. **Page 53.** *George Brinton McClellan,* (1826–1885), photograph, Frederick Gutekunst, Library of Congress Manuscript Division. **Page 54.** *Lloyd H. Hall Co. Map of Virginia*, created and published in New York circa 1862, Library of Congress Geography and Map Division. This map shows battlefields underlined in red. **Page 57.** *Brigadier General Richard Stoddart Ewell* (1817–1872), photograph circa 1861, © Medford Historical Society Collection/CORBIS. **Page 58.** View of Winchester, Virginia, pencil drawing, July 20, 1862, Edwin Forbes (1839–1895), Prints and Photographs Division, Library of Congress. View is from the fort on the hill northeast of the town, the breastwork can be seen in foreground. **Page 61.** *Battle of Cross Keys*, watercolor sketch, Private Henry Berckhoff, 8th New York, The Gilder Lehrman Collection, on deposit at the Pierpont Morgan Library. **Page 64.** *"Stonewall Jackson's Way,"* sheet music, 1862, Miller & Beacham, John Williamson Palmer lyricist, Conf. Music #158, Duke University, Rare Book, Manuscript, and Special Collections Library. **Page 66.** *General Robert E. Lee* (1807–1870), photograph, 1863, Julian Vannerson, Library of Congress Prints and Photographs Division. **Page 70.** *Battle of Malvern Hill*, July 1, 1862, Private Robert Knox Sneden, Virginia Historical Society. **Pages 74–75.** *The Slaughters Mountain* (Cedar Mountain), drawing, created and published between 1861 and 1865, by Edwin Forbes, Prints and Photographs Division, Library of Congress. **Page 78.** *The battle of Groveton* (Second Battle of Bull Run), drawing, Edwin Forbes, Prints and Photographs Division, Library of Congress. **Page 77.** *General John Pope* (1822–1892), photograph, Mathew Brady of the Mathew Brady Studio, Still Picture Branch, National Archives and Records Administration. **Pages 82–83.** *The stone bridge over Antietam Creek*, photograph created September 1862, published circa 1866, Alexander Gardner (1821–1882), Prints and Photographs Division, Library of Congress. **Page 85.** *Mary Anna and Julia Jackson* (1862–1889), photograph Virginia Military Institute Archives. **Page 87.** *Bringing the wounded into Fredericksburg in the afternoon—of Saturday*, pencil drawing on tan paper, circa December 1862, Arthur Lumley (1837?–1912). Prints and Photographs Division, Library of Congress. **Page 89.** *Major General Joseph Hooker* (1814–1879), photograph, created and published between 1860 and 1865, Brady National Photographic Art Gallery in Washington, D.C., Prints and Photographs Division, Library of Congress. **Page 93.** *Chancellorsville*, engraving, May 1–3, 1863, Alfred R. Waud, © CORBIS. In this engraving, Union general Darius N. Couch's corps form a line of battle in the fields at Chancellorsville to cover the retreat of the Eleventh Corps. **Page 96.** *Thomas Jackson*, etching circa 1863, Adalbert J. Volck (1828–1912), after the death mask created by Frederick Volck, National Portrait Gallery, Smithsonian Institution. **Page 98.** *Women mourning at the grave of Thomas J. "Stonewall" Jackson*, photograph, circa 1866, Boude & Miley, Virginia Military Institute Archives. The women in this photograph are not identified, although they may have been students at a local girls' school.

Credits

Photo Credits

Cover, pp. 26, 28, 29, 36, 85, 98 Virginia Military Institute Archives; cover (background), pp. 9, 19, 38, 41, 49, 50, 58, 66, 74–75, 78, 82–83, 87, 89 Prints and Photographs Division, Library of Congress; p. 4 © The Corcoran Gallery of Art/CORBIS; pp. 8, 10, 23, 33 courtesy of the Stonewall Jackson House; pp. 14, 15 West Point Museum Art Collection, United States Military Academy; p. 21 The Randy Haynie Family Collection and the Louisiana Old State Capitol Center for Political and Governmental History; p. 31 Rockbridge Historical Society, Photograph Collection. Special Collections, Leyburn Library, Washington and Lee University, Lexington, Virginia; pp. 35, 40, 96 National Portrait Gallery, Smithsonian Institution/Art Resource, NY; pp. 42, 46 (left), 47, 77 Still Picture Branch, National Archives and Records Administration; p. 45 Division of the History of Technology, Armed Forces History, National Museum of American History, S.I.; p. 46 (right) The Museum of the Confederacy, Richmond, VA; p. 48 Valentine Richmond History Center; p. 57 © Medford Historical Society Collection/CORBIS; pp. 52, 70 Virginia Historical Society; p. 53 Library of Congress Manuscript Division; pp. 54, 67 Library of Congress Geography and Map Division; p. 61 The Gilder Lehrman Collection, on deposit at the Pierpont Morgan Library; p. 64 Duke University, Rare Book, Manuscript, and Special Collections Library; p. 91 the Museum of the Confederacy, Richmond, Virginia, photography by Katherine Wetzel; p. 93 © CORBIS; p. 99 © Kevin Fleming/CORBIS.

Project Editors
Gillian Houghton and Jennifer Way

Series Design
Laura Murawski

Layout Design
Corinne L. Jacob

Photo Researcher
Jeffrey Wendt